P9-DBM-068

A Cultural History
of the
United States

■

Through the Decades

The 1950s

Stuart A. Kallen

Lucent Books, Inc., San Diego, California

Contents

Introduction

A family enjoys a program on a black-and-white console television. The television set became affordable and widely available in the 1950s, dramatically altering American culture and leisure time.

The Black-and-White Decade

Images of the 1950s are recorded in countless black-and-white photographs, movies, and early television programs. It seems fitting those memories are preserved in black and white because the fifties was a time of stark contrasts. On one hand, the U.S. economy was booming. Millions of optimistic, mostly male, single-wage earners were supporting families, buying houses and new cars, and sending their kids to college. On the other

hand, the prospect of instant nuclear annihilation led to generalized anxiety and fear of the future.

These contrasts were also reflected in the social mores of the day. The fear of world communist takeover spawned public suspicion and rejection of anything that was different or strange, and prompted strict conformity of dress and manners in America. At the same time black rhythm and blues music merged with white country music to foment a rock 'n' roll music rebellion. But while black roots music was popular among white teenagers, black people were denied equal rights and justice. In America's South, African Americans were forced to live in separate neighborhoods, attend separate schools, eat in separate restaurants, and sleep in separate hotels.

The Influence of World War II

The fifties, of course, was an outgrowth of the forties, an era of world war and the widespread destruction of Europe and Asia. The conflict killed 50 million people and shattered the political structure of Europe. Though the United States was spared physical destruction, when the bombs of World War II stopped falling in 1945, it faced a world profoundly different from the world of 1939. The former Axis powers of Germany, Italy, and Japan were crushed. Although the Soviet Union suffered more than 20 million casualties, both civilian and military, it emerged with the largest standing army in world history.

The United States had ended the war with Japan by dropping atomic bombs on the cities of Hiroshima and Nagasaki. Those two weapons, the

A homeless family walks through the ruins of their European village during World War II. While Europe was physically and economically devastated during the war, the United States remained relatively unscathed.

first use of so-called weapons of mass destruction, killed over 75,000 people and seriously wounded countless others. Not long after, the secrets of the atomic bomb fell into Soviet hands, and a new term—cold war—was coined to describe building postwar tensions.

As Europe rebuilt from the ruins, the United States emerged as the

American servicemen survey the ruins of Hiroshima after the atomic bomb blast. The atomic bomb thrust the world into the nuclear age and ultimately led to a dangerous competition between the United States and the Soviet Union to stockpile the weapon.

strongest and wealthiest country on earth—a world superpower for the first time. But under Soviet dictator Joseph Stalin, the USSR took control of Eastern Europe and North Korea, developed its own atomic weapons program, and challenged the United States for world domination. The two superpowers began to stockpile nuclear weapons at an unprecedented rate. The A-bomb was abandoned in favor of the hydrogen bomb, with one hundred times more destructive power. The nuclear standoff was likened to two schoolchildren standing up to their knees in gasoline playing with matches while the world held its collective breath.

A New Prosperity

After the trauma of the Great Depression of the 1930s and the global conflict of the 1940s, people everywhere longed to exercise freedom in economic rather than political or social terms. Everyone seemed to strive for middle-class, material well-being. Security meant finding a white-collar job with a large company, getting married, having children, and moving to the newly built suburbs.

Few white Americans doubted the goodness of their society. Americans trusted their politicians to tell the truth and do the right thing. The nation's vast wealth was shared by more people than ever before, and provided a prosperity beyond the wildest dreams of earlier generations.

Cracks in the Veneer

But as the fifties came to a close, cracks developed in this veneer. African Americans, who had fought side by side with white Americans during World War II, were denied their piece of the American Dream. Young people, whose numbers exploded in the postwar baby boom, grew bored and restless. Rock 'n' roll music offered teenagers a new way to rebel against their parents. Below the surface, the fifties was more exciting and more rebellious than the happy faces represented on the new medium of television suggested.

The legacy of the fifties is still with us in many ways. The cold war and the threat of communist takeover are long gone. But television and radio still shower us daily with Elvis Presley, Buddy Holly, *I Love Lucy,* and other images of the fifties culture.

A new father views his newborn child through the window of a hospital nursery. The 1950s would see a vast split between the postwar baby-boom generation and their parents, resulting in a generation gap that would be duplicated in later generations.

Thousands of Internet home pages are dedicated to fifties icons from actor James Dean to UNIVAC, the world's first business computer.

The fifties was a decade of contrasts—communism versus capitalism, black versus white, conformity versus rock rebellion, all a mere two generations ago. The baby boomers born then are today's world leaders; thus, the men and women shaped by the fifties will lead the way into the twenty-first century.

Immediately following World War II, the Soviet Union used its vast resources to invade and take over the nations of Eastern Europe. These actions led to the lengthy conflict known as the cold war.

Superpowers and the Cold War

In the summer of 1945, Great Britain, the United States, and the USSR celebrated their joint victory over Nazi Germany and Japan. A new international organization, the United Nations, was created in a hopeful attempt to lead the world into a permanent era of world peace and cooperation. That hope did not last into the 1950s. Soviet leader Joseph Stalin considered capitalism to be the main enemy of communism. He loudly warned the Western democracies that he had every intention of fighting that enemy. To that end, his regime set up satellite states in Eastern Europe, Asia, and the emerging countries of the developing world.

President Harry S. Truman

Vice President Harry Truman became president of the United States on April

12, 1945, at the death of President Franklin D. Roosevelt. The no-nonsense Democrat was a direct contrast to the elegant and aristocratic Roosevelt. Truman was blunt, open, and unintimidated. People saw him as a rugged man from a small town, a typical American. As president he was accused (by Republicans in the opposing party) as turning the White House over to "Missouri roughnecks and poker-playing back-room operators who drank bourbon and told off-color jokes." [1]

True, Truman was not an average politician. He neither flattered nor responded to flattery. He did not like "stuffed shirts" and "fuddy-duddies" who used "two-dollar words" or "weasel words." His experiences in the military made him wary of generals and he called the diplomats in the State Department the "striped-pants boys."

Unlike most presidents, Truman had no personal fortune. He never went to college and his family had always lived modestly. But Truman had a sterling record for honesty. "Three things ruin a man," he liked to say, "power, money, and women. I never wanted power, I never had any money, and the only woman in my life is [my wife] up at the house right now." [2]

Harry S. Truman took over the presidency after Franklin Roosevelt's death in 1945. Truman posed a marked contrast to the aristocratic Roosevelt.

Hot War to Cold War

After World War II, Truman quickly approved American military and economic aid to rebuild Western Europe. He also sanctioned aid to countries, like Greece, that were threatened by communist takeover. In the meantime, the Soviets successfully exploded their own atomic bomb on September 23,1949. The blast not

Europe During the Cold War

Denmark
Netherlands
Britain
Berlin
East Germany
Poland
Belgium
Luxembourg
West Germany
Czechoslovakia
Switzerland
Austria
Hungary
France
Italy
Romania
Yugoslavia
Spain
Albania
USSR

Soviet-Controlled
Eastern Europe

Soviet Union that lasted until 1989. The battle was waged in the decades following World War II by any means short of direct military conflict. But the threat of direct conflict loomed large in people's lives—especially in the fifties. During that decade, the superpowers amassed a stockpile of nuclear weapons capable of annihilating the world ten times over in less than thirty minutes. This standoff led to indirect confrontations as the superpowers competed for world markets and political influence.

The USSR installed Communist governments in Poland, Czechoslovakia, and East Germany between 1946 and 1948. Winston Churchill, the British prime minister, accused Stalin of dropping an "iron curtain" to cordon off Eastern Europe. In response, the United States, Britain, France, and nine other countries created the North Atlantic Treaty Organization (NATO) for mutual defense and strategic military planning. The United States, under the provisions of the Marshall Plan, pumped $17 billion into rebuilding war-torn Western Europe. And U.S. armed forces maintained a military occupation of much of Western Europe and parts of Asia immediately after the war.

only ended the American monopoly on the bomb, but ushered in a new age of covert warfare and worldwide dread that became known as the cold war. The United States had no contingency plans for this event. A huge Soviet army was stationed at the very heart of central Europe. Western Europe and the United States were busy disarming from World War II at what military men considered an alarming rate. Air force commander Curtis LeMay warned, "The era when we might have destroyed Russia completely and not even skinned our elbows doing it has ended." [3]

Cold war is the term given to the economic and ideological conflict between the United States and the

The Central Intelligence Agency

Despite Truman's efforts, communism continued to spread, and the cold war intensified. Because the United States and the USSR maintained diplomatic relations, the United States refrained from overt, or open, warlike actions. Few such restraints governed covert, or secret, confrontations between the East-West rivals. In December 1947, Truman signed the National Security Act, creating, among other things, the Central Intelligence Agency (CIA). The official mission of the CIA was to gather information about Soviet movements in foreign countries. But the scope of Central Intelligence was broadened considerably to include direct intervention in the politics and economies of sovereign nations. As Walter Hixson writes in his book *Parting the Curtain*:

> Citing the "vicious covert activities of the USSR, the CIA was authorized to create a covert operations branch for which "the U.S. government can plausibly disclaim any responsibility."

The measures short of war to be employed included "propaganda; economic warfare; preventative direct action, including sabotage, anti-sabotage, demolition, and evacuation measures; subversion against hostile states, including assistance to underground resistance movements, guerrillas and refugee liberation groups, and support of indigenous anti-communist elements in threatened countries of the free world." Legislation approved in 1949 authorized the CIA to spend money at the director's discretion, exempting it from requirements that it be accountable to Congress. Funds for covert operations increased from $4.7 million in 1949 to $82 million in 1952.

The covert policies of the CIA were not revealed for many years. But the policy of using extralegal means to subvert the governments of sovereign nations has been subject to serious criticism—and untold casualties—over the years.

A-Bombs and H-Bombs

The United States also countered security threats by attempting to build bigger and better weapons, notably the first detonated hydrogen bomb, or H-bomb, in 1952. Most scientific breakthroughs are celebrated; this one was not. One scientist who witnessed the blast said, "In the last milli-second of the earth's existence—the last men will see what we saw."[4] Physicist J. Robert Oppenheimer, director of the atomic bomb project, said, "You will believe that this undertaking has not been without its misgivings; they are heavy on us today, when the future, which has so many elements of high promise, is yet only a stone's throw from despair."[5]

Someone asked Albert Einstein,

An impressive array of rocket launchers passes through an open plaza in a show of Soviet military might. In the years following World War II, both the United States and the USSR set about stockpiling weapons as insurance against future attack.

whose formulas led to the development of the bomb, how World War III would be fought. Einstein glumly answered that he had no idea what kind of weapons would be used in the Third World War, but he could assure the questioner that "the war after that will be fought with stones." [6]

These comments were not exaggerations. The H-bomb delivered the explosive equivalent of 1 million tons of TNT. In the entire five years of World War II, combatants had used the cumulative equivalent of only 3 million tons of TNT.

In 1953, Soviet premier Georgi Malenkov (briefly, Stalin's successor) announced, "The Soviet government deems it necessary to report that the United States has *no monopoly* in the production of the hydrogen bomb." [7] Malenkov's announcement put the world on notice that the Soviets, too, had exploded an H-bomb.

The development of nuclear weapons led to a stalemate between the superpowers based on deterrence. Both countries believed that if one launched an attack, the other would instantly retaliate, and a chain reaction of detonations would be inevitable. The United States, the USSR, and the entire planet would be destroyed. The dangerous balance designed to prevent this scenario, known as mutually assured destruction, or MAD, forced the superpowers to forge and support alliances in Europe, Africa, Asia, and South America economically and ideologically. Both sides also loaded their military bases with nuclear weapons, just in case.

American Reaction to Nuclear Weapons

Nuclear weapons were widely and immediately accepted by the popular press in the fifties, in such articles as "Atomic Weapons Will Save Money." *Look* magazine cheerily pointed out that A-bombs were "one of the cheapest forms of destruction known to man." [8]

Average Americans also had strong opinions about atomic weapons. The general view was that the differences between the Soviet and American systems were unresolvable and that nuclear weaponry, once invented, would never go away. Many Americans believed that the Soviets

had less to lose and would therefore launch a surprise attack on the United States. After wiping out North America, went this reasoning, the Soviets would rule the world.

A 1950 Gallup poll reflected this paranoia. Seventy percent of those surveyed believed the Soviet Union wanted to rule the world. Forty-one percent felt the United States would fight another war within five years. Seventy-five percent stated that they feared American cities would be bombed in the next war. Nineteen percent felt the next war would wipe out the entire human race.

Communists in China, War in Korea

Fear of communist world takeover seemed even more real due to other world events. China fell to Mao Zedong's communist forces in 1949. After China became a communist nation, more than one-quarter of the world's people—close to 500 million Chinese and 220 million Soviets— lived under communist rule. This made many Americans even more afraid. They knew very little about Chinese history or the corruption of former leader Chiang Kai-shek. Many blamed Truman, who had defeated Thomas Dewey in the 1948 presidential election, for China's fall.

Nuclear Contamination

The cold war arms race was responsible for releasing nuclear fallout across the globe. More than two hundred nuclear tests were performed in the Nevada desert beginning in 1950. In one accident, hundreds of sheep died of radiation poisoning. In later years, residents of nearby towns had a higher than expected incidence of leukemia and other cancers. Scientists knew the hazard of radioactive fallout, but average citizens were not alerted to the danger.

When the H-bomb was invented, the United States moved its tests to islands in the South Pacific. On March 1, 1954, 25 members of the Japanese fishing vessel *Lucky Dragon* saw the predawn sky bathed in a brilliant light, followed by a huge shock wave and a giant mushroom cloud. The unlucky men on the *Lucky Dragon* witnessed the first explosion of an H-bomb on Bikini Atoll. All were stricken with radiation sickness, as were 239 residents of the Marshall Islands and 28 American military personnel. As in other H-bomb blasts, more than seven thousand square miles of ocean were contaminated with radiation from the blast. The radioactive fish from the *Lucky*

A nuclear test is conducted offshore Bikini Atoll. Unfortunately, ignorance of the effects of such tests left islanders and military personnel dangerously exposed to high levels of radiation.

Dragon reached Japanese markets. When the army warned that the fish were contaminated the country panicked. Millions of tons of recently caught fish were buried and the entire staple of the Japanese diet was suspect.

Also in 1958, a small hydrogen test on the Pacific island of Runit misfired and spread dangerous plutonium all over the island. The site is contaminated to this day.

In part due to this criticism, Truman did take action in another conflict involving communism. Japan brutally ruled Korea from 1905 until the end of World War II. After the war, the country was divided, occupied in the northern half by the Soviets and in the southern half by the United States. Each half desperately wanted to take over the other. The Soviets ended their occupation in 1949 but left behind a well-trained North Korean army. The United States also pulled out in 1949, but left little weaponry behind.

North Korea invaded South Korea,

in June 1950, starting a war in a desolate, harsh land that the United States was loath to enter. Temperatures could reach 104°F in the summer and minus 40°F in the winter. Korea had often been a battleground between China, Russia, and Japan but held little strategic interest for the United States. In fact, most Americans had barely even heard of Korea.

The United Nations authorized the United States to lead UN troops to defend South Korea. Truman called the confrontation a "United Nations police action" instead of a war. Secretary of State Dean Acheson summed up the Korean problem when he said, "If the best minds in the world had set out to find us in the worst possible location in the world to fight this damnable war, politically and militarily, the unanimous choice would have been Korea." [9]

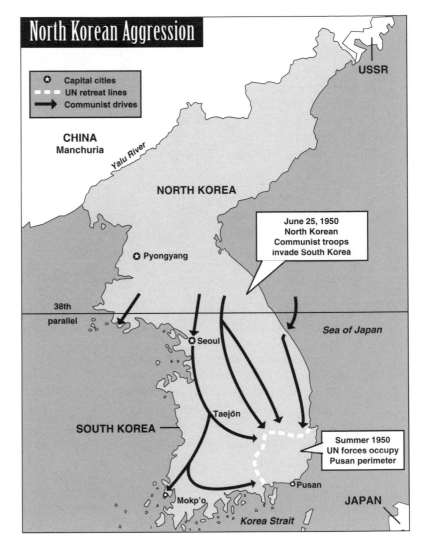

North Korean Aggression

- ✪ Capital cities
- - - - UN retreat lines
- ➤ Communist drives

CHINA
Manchuria

Yalu River

USSR

NORTH KOREA

✪ Pyongyang

38th parallel

June 25, 1950
North Korean
Communist troops
invade South Korea

Sea of Japan

✪ Seoul

Taejŏn

SOUTH KOREA

Summer 1950
UN forces occupy
Pusan perimeter

○ Pusan

○ Mokp'o

JAPAN

Korea Strait

From the beginning, the war was a disaster. The better-trained and better-equipped North Korean forces almost pushed the UN troops out of South Korea in the first six weeks of fighting. In the winter of 1950–1951, General Douglas MacArthur sent Americans deep into the north not realizing they

American military police take into custody a North Korean communist sympathizer. Known as the "Forgotten War," the Korean War quickly became unpopular with the American people.

did not have the weapons or clothing to withstand the bitter cold temperatures. Near the Chinese border the Americans faced a million well-armed, warmly dressed Chinese soldiers. The United States suffered heavy and humiliating losses, fighting in temperatures bottoming out at minus 30°F. The battered Americans were forced to retreat.

At home, people began calling Korea "the no-win war," "Truman's war," and "the Democrats' war." U.S. senators went on television and radio and demanded that Truman use atomic bombs in Korea and even on Red China. Americans were forced to face the very real possibility of World War III.

Truman dismissed MacArthur, who supported an invasion of China. MacArthur was replaced by General Matthew Ridgway, and the Soviets agreed to negotiate a cease-fire in 1951. The agreement took two years to complete. In the meantime, the shooting went on and casualties grew by the thousands. The conflict lasted a little more than three years. Overall, 103,000 Americans were wounded and 54,246 were killed in the Korean "police action."

Unlike World War II, the Korean War was the subject of few movies, books, and plays. Returning veterans were not given the hero's welcome that World War II vets had received. If there was one positive effect of the war, it was that for the first time, the U.S. military became racially integrated. (African Americans fought bravely in America's other wars, but in separate, or segregated, units.) In Korea, Frank L. Petersen became the highest-ranking African American in the marines and the first black marine pilot, flying sixty-four successful combat missions.

The dissatisfaction with the Korean War and other foreign policy issues made the American people even less confident in Truman as a president. In 1952, Republican Dwight D. Eisenhower, a World War II hero known as "Ike" was elected president by a landslide. Richard Nixon, a congressman from California, was his vice president. Eisenhower quickly became one of the most popular presidents in history, serving two terms.

A U.S. infantryman is consoled by a comrade after one of his friends was killed during the Korean War. The United States suffered a large number of casualties and troops were unprepared for the terrain and weather in Korea.

Power Shift in the USSR

When Soviet leader Joseph Stalin died of a brain hemorrhage in 1953, Americans were fearful that someone worse would take his place. Author I. F. Stone wrote in March 1953:

If Stalin was the aggressive monster painted in official propaganda, his death should have cheered Washington. Actually, the unspoken premise of American policy has been that Stalin was so anxious for peace he would do nothing unless Soviet soil were violated.

Hungarian revolutionaries pose for a photograph in 1956. The Soviet Union brutally crushed the revolution, leaving twenty-five thousand dead.

With his death, the baiting of the Russian bear—the favorite sport of American politics—suddenly seemed dangerous. [Congressman] Martin Dies rose in the House to say that while Stalin was "utterly cruel and ruthless, he was more conservative than the younger Bolsheviks [Communists]. Few would have dared a week earlier to dwell on the conservative and cautious temperament of the Soviet ruler, much less imply that this was favorable to world stability and peace. [10]

Nikita Khrushchev soon emerged as the power in the Communist Party and Soviet government. His early actions led Americans to hope for a thaw in the cold war; Khrushchev released about 8 million of the 13 million political prisoners in Stalin's system of Soviet prison camps. Khrushchev also instigated a campaign to remove Stalin's name from monuments, cities, and street names.

Under Khrushchev, the Soviet Union faced revolutions in the nations it controlled. In 1956 thousands of students and workers marched for freedom in Hungary, which had been under Soviet domination since 1946. The protesters, urged on by the U.S.-backed Radio Free Europe, tore down statues of Stalin and declared independence from the Soviet Union. The protests ended a few weeks later when fifteen Soviet Red Army divisions entered Hungary with five thousand tanks. After the revolt was crushed, twenty-five thousand Hungarians lay dead, and several hundred thousand more had been forced to flee the country. Khrushchev's actions quickly made him the new villain to the Western world.

Eisenhower Comes to Power

The world events of the fifties left most people anxious and scared. It was hard to ignore Chinese politics and Soviet tanks in Hungary when the world was sitting on a tinderbox of atomic weapons. Americans desperately wanted to live in a safe world.

But communism was not confined to Russia, China, or Korea; Americans feared communists right in their own

The Soviet *Sputnik*

On October 5, 1957, Americans awoke to the news that the Soviet Union had successfully launched a satellite into orbit around the earth. The 184-pound device, called *Sputnik,* carried a radio transmitter. *Sputnik* emitted a beeping sound for two weeks before its batteries ran down.

A navy rear admiral said: "*Sputnik* is a hunk of iron anybody could launch." But the average person in the street quickly realized that if the Soviets could fire a "hunk of iron" so easily into space, they could also drop a bomb into America's backyard.

In the United States, former Nazi rocket scientist Wernher von Braun was working on an American version of *Sputnik.* After a few aborted attempts, the United States launched *Explorer I* in 1958. It was the first U.S. satellite to go into orbit and it established Cape Canaveral in Florida as America's primary launching pad. Von Braun continued to work on launching a man into space. The United States achieved that goal—after the Soviets—when Alan Shepard Jr. rode von Braun's Mercury rocket into orbit in 1961.

hometowns. While Americans seemed powerless to stop communism abroad, they were determined to do something about it in their own country. The bombs of the USSR and China soon set off a firestorm of paranoia and hysteria in the United States.

Chapter Two

Americans protest against communism outside the Waldorf-Astoria in New York. With the USSR's aggressive takeover of Eastern European nations and its quick development of its own atom bomb, many U.S. citizens believed that communism was a threat at home as well.

The Cold War at Home

With Communism taking hold in Asia, Eastern Europe, and developing countries of Africa and the Carribean, Americans had reason to be fearful. With two of the world's largest countries—China and the Soviet Union—under communist dictatorships, a hostile takeover of the United States seemed possible. Thousands of Americans had joined the Communist Party during the dark days of the Great Depression when poverty and massive unemployment suggested capitalism was failing. In the fifties, these people became suspects, even after many renounced their communist beliefs as youthful experimentation. Scientists and technicians who had worked on atomic bombs also came under suspicion when the Soviets developed their own weapons. Investigations exposing a

Library of Congress Cataloging-in-Publication Data

Kallen, Stuart A., 1955-
  The 1950s / by Stuart A. Kallen.
      p.   cm. — (A cultural history of the United States through
  the decades)
      Includes bibliographical references and index.
      Summary: Discusses the political, economic, and cultural life of
  the United States in the 1950s, including the effects of the cold
  war, the civil rights movement, television, music, art, science, and
  technology.
      ISBN 1-56006-555-9 (lib. : alk. paper)
      1. United States—History—1933-1945—Juvenile literature.
  2. United States—History—1945-1953—Juvenile literature.
  3. United States—Social life and customs—1918-1945—Juvenile
  literature. 4. United States-—Social life and customs—1945-1970-
  -Juvenile literature. 5. Nineteen fifties—Juvenile literature.
  [1. Nineteen fifties. 2. United States—History—1945-1953.
  3. United States—History—1953-1961. 4. United States–Social life
  customs—1918-1945. 5. United States—Social life and customs—
  1945-1970.] I. Title. II. Series.
  E813.K33   1999   98-26669
  973.921—dc21   CIP
                                                       AC

Copyright 1999 by Lucent Books, Inc.
P.O. Box 289011, San Diego, California 92198-9011

Printed in the U.S.A.

handful of people as spies in fact convinced Americans that thousands more must live among them.

Many politicians, especially Republicans, took advantage of the "Red scare" to further their own political ends, accusing Truman, the Democrats, and liberals in general of being "soft" on communism. The truth was not necessarily of primary importance in this red-baiting, and the fact that there was *some* credibility to *some* accusations fueled the fear.

Fear and hatred of communists rose to a fever pitch. Anyone who did not fit into the status quo image of white, middle-class, Anglo-Saxon America risked being labeled a "Commie." That included black people fighting for equal rights, Jews, intellectuals, union organizers, immigrants, college professors, artists, musicians, poets, and others.

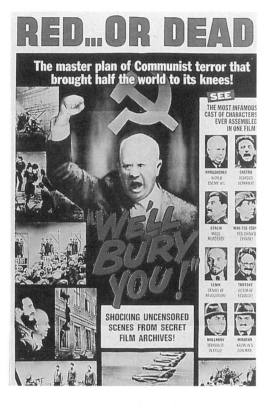

An anticommunist propaganda poster emphasizes a threat to the United States. During the 1950s, many innocent people were accused of being communists.

The Red Scare and the Media

Many Americans were convinced that thousands of communists infiltrated the echelons of government and Hollywood. For the most part, the media magnified their fears. Major magazines ran articles with titles such as "Communists Penetrate Wall Street," "Russian Spies: Trained to Raise Hell in America," "Reds Are After Your Child," and "How Communists Take Over."[11] Books with anticommunist themes became best-sellers. Hollywood joined the fray with movies such as *I Married a Communist, The Red Menace,* and *I Was a Communist for the FBI.*

America's newest villain was drawn in cartoons as a vodka-swilling, jackbooted communist in a long overcoat and furry hat. Communists were portrayed as devious fiends who could hypnotize ordinary people into becoming their unwilling dupes.

These views were expressed none too subtly by one of the most popular fictional characters of the time, detective Mike Hammer. In Mickey Spillane's 1951 detective novel, *In One Lonely Night,* Hammer brags,

> I killed more people tonight than I have fingers on my hands. I shot them in cold blood and enjoyed every minute of it. They were Commies. They were red sons-of-bitches who should have died a long time ago. They never thought there were people like me in this country. They figured us to all be as soft as horse manure and just as stupid. [12]

Spillane sold millions of similar pulp fiction detective novels. In 1956, of the ten best-selling novels in America, seven featured Spillane's Mike Hammer.

The Cold War Economy

Historically, mass movements of hatred come most often when a country is stressed economically. During hard times, people are more willing to find an enemy to blame for their problems. But, the Red scare of the fifties took place during a booming American economy. And, ironically, it was an economy that was booming because of the cold war.

The demand for high-tech weapons of the day created hundreds of new businesses. As the fifties dawned, sophisticated factories opened to build defense technology such as jet aircraft, rockets, ships, and submarines, and produce new synthetic materials such as nylon and plastic. Many technological advancements originally developed for the military were applied to consumer items.

Consumers were also spending at a fever pitch. When soldiers returned from the war they were given opportunities by the so-called GI Bill, which provided cheap college education and no-money-down, low interest home loans. Almost 8 million veterans were suddenly eligible to get a good job, buy their first home, fill it full of modern electrical appliances, and park a new car in the driveway.

The Korean War also had a strong effect on the American economy. Because industries were once again focused on arms production, there were shortages of consumer goods from tires to televisions. But at the same time, defense contractors were hiring workers at an unprecedented rate to build B-52 bombers, guided missiles, and hydrogen bombs. After the Korean War, Congress authorized even more defense spending to fight communism and—incidentally—to fuel the fifties economy.

Spies Among Us?

Anticommunist hysteria grew in 1949, when a State Department official named Alger Hiss was accused of passing important State Department documents to Soviet agents in the 1930s. Hiss denied all charges and claimed that he was being framed by the Federal Bureau of Investigation, or FBI.

Because more than seven years had passed since Hiss's alleged crimes, he could not be put on trial for treason. Instead he was tried and convicted of perjury on January 21, 1950. Hiss was given a five-year sentence, but he maintained his innocence.

In 1950, German-born scientist Dr. Klaus Fuchs, then living in Britain, was tried on charges that he gave atomic secrets to the Soviets. Fuchs had worked on the original atom bomb project and admitted that he had given away top-secret information. England was embarrassed by the Fuchs case and rushed it through the legal system—his trial lasted only ninety minutes. Fuchs was convicted and sentenced to fourteen years in prison. It was clear that security of the American atom bomb project had

Dr. Klaus Fuchs was tried and convicted of passing atomic secrets to the Soviet Union.

been compromised by Fuchs.

The Fuchs affair triggered an investigation into his colleagues and acquaintances in America, which led to the arrest of chemist Harry Gold, machinist David Greenglass, and Greenglass's wife, Ruth. Among others arrested were Greenglass's sister and brother-in-law Ethel and Julius Rosenberg.

The arrest of this alleged spy ring was a media sensation in America. Because all the defendants happened to be Jewish, millions of people imagined an international Jewish conspiracy supposedly spreading communism, and blamed this conspiracy for the

Nazis Come to America

When World War II ended, victorious American intelligence teams began a hunt for German military and scientific booty such as rocket and aircraft designs, medicines, and electronics. They were also hunting for the most precious "treasure" of all: the scientists whose work had nearly won the war for Germany—the engineers, researchers, and intelligence officers of the Nazi war machine. U.S. law explicitly prohibited Nazi officials from immigrating to America, but, as Tom Bower writes in his book, *The Paperclip Conspiracy: The Hunt for Nazi Scientists:*

> German scientists were identified simply with an ordinary paperclip on their personal file. Like so many other beneficiaries of the "Paperclip" conspiracy, they would become respectable American citizens, their wartime activities notwithstanding, because senior military officers determined that, in the national interest, American immigration laws should be willfully ignored.

Notable among these men were:

Arthur Rudolph, operations director of the Mittelwerk factory at the Dora-Nordhausen concentration camps, where twenty thousand workers died from beatings, hangings, and starvation. Rudolph became a U.S. citizen and later designed the *Saturn 5* rocket used in the Apollo moon landings.

Wernher von Braun, who from 1937 to 1945 was the technical director of the Peenemunde rocket research center, where the V-2 rocket—which devasted England—was developed. Von Braun worked on guided missles for the U.S. Army and was later director of NASA's Marshall Space Flight Center.

General Reinhard Gehlen, a Nazi zealot who had overseen notorious crimes during the war—the torture, interrogation, and murder by starvation of some 4 million Soviet prisoners. Gehlen and his SS unit were hired as agents of the CIA.

problems facing the United States. And the source was not Soviets across the vast ocean—it was right under their own noses. Ethel and Julius Rosenberg were from New York City; in the 1930s, they were members of the American Communist Party.

Harry Gold, arrested in connection with Fuchs's case, claimed to have passed secrets to David Greenglass. Greenglass claimed he was recruited by Julius Rosenberg, who was arrested and imprisoned. Ethel was called before a grand jury, arrested, and illegally held for eight months without being charged with a crime. Ruth Greenglass claimed Ethel typed information brought to Julius from David. The Rosenbergs steadfastly denied they were spies.

The government's case against Ethel was weakened by the fact that there was no evidence of any typed documents. But she was an admitted leftist and the prosecutors wanted to use her to implicate her husband. The Rosenbergs were tried, convicted, and sentenced to death in 1951.

The Rosenbergs died in the electric chair on June 19, 1953. They left behind two young sons. To this day, the guilt or innocence of the Rosenbergs—especially Ethel—is unproven.

Hunting Reds with the FBI

The Rosenbergs and other accused spies became the all-encompassing obsession of FBI chief J. Edgar Hoover. Hoover began harassing suspected communists after World War II. He believed that fully one-third of the world's population was part of a great communist conspiracy. Hoover's FBI agents tapped telephones, followed suspects, planted informants, and compiled files on millions of unsuspecting Americans.

John Edgar Hoover was one of the most powerful men in America in the fifties. His name alone struck fear in the hearts of even the most popular politicians. With wiretaps and clandestine photographs, Hoover com-

Ethel and Julian Rosenberg are delivered to separate jails in 1951. Tried and convicted of spying for the Soviet Union, the extent of the Rosenbergs' guilt, especially Ethel's, is still questioned.

piled damaging files on many powerful men. The files contained proof of sexual liaisons and money changing hands illegally. Hoover used this information to control individuals from common citizens to the president. As David Halberstam writes:

> Because he was the keeper of the files, he was a man not to be

FBI director J. Edgar Hoover far surpassed his legal powers by wiretapping and photographing government officials and private citizens in his pursuit of communists.

crossed. He dealt in fear. In the inner circle of Washington, the very powerful (almost all of whom had in some way or another transgressed—sexually or financially) feared what his files contained on them; his appropriations [budgets for the FBI] went through Congress ever more readily. [13]

When Eisenhower was elected, Hoover's power could not be curbed by even the president. There were no constitutional limits on his authority and the average congressman so feared the contents of his files that the Congress would not reprimand him. The House Subcommittee on the Judiciary reported in 1972 that the bureau held 883 current files on senators and 722 current files on congressmen.

Joe McCarthy's Fictional List of Commies

While Hoover was compiling files on politicians, another government official was threatening to make public other secrets. In February 1950, a little-known Republican senator from Wisconsin gave a speech in Wheeling, West Virginia. In his remarks to the Women's Republican Club, Senator Joseph McCarthy almost casually mentioned that there were communists in the State Department, and that they controlled U.S. foreign policy. In the middle of the speech, McCarthy said:

While I cannot take the time to name all the men in the State Department who have been named as members of the

Communist Party and members of a spy ring I have here in my hand a list of 205 that were known to the Secretary of State as being members of the Communist Party and who nevertheless are still working and shaping the policy of the State Department. [14]

McCarthy punctuated his announcement by waving a piece of paper that he claimed listed the 205 names. (It was actually his own laundry list, but no one knew that.)

This accusation was common grousing among Republicans, and McCarthy himself had no idea that his speech would have so explosive an effect. "Otherwise," speculated reporter Willard Edwards, "he would have taken along a right-wing reporter to help tutor him and write his speeches . . . and he would have picked a bigger town than Wheeling." [15] In any case, the story moved over the Associated Press (AP) wires and became headline news the next morning. Although McCarthy never showed his supposed list to anyone, the fear-mongering known as the McCarthy era had begun.

McCarthy gave the same speech the next night in Salt Lake City, Utah. This time he claimed he had the names of "57 card-carrying Communists" [16] in the State Department. The number of communist infiltrators kept changing and there was a vagueness to the charges. One reporter was sure it was a show: McCarthy didn't care about communists; he simply loved the attention—and campaign contributions—that followed.

The McCarthy Witch-Hunts

Before long McCarthy had the attention of the entire nation. He took his charges to the Senate, where he held the floor for six straight hours. He raged and accused, demanding the Senate indict people on his list. The Senate—increasingly fearful of looking soft on communism—responded, establishing a special investigation team to track down every one of McCarthy's leads. (Most of the individuals on the list were communists in the 1930s whose names were secretly fed to McCarthy by Hoover.) For months, the Senate sorted evidence and listened to testimony. Its conclusion? Not one of McCarthy's accusations turned out to be true. All his cases were the result of lies, gossip, and rumor. The committee labeled McCarthy's charges a hoax and a fraud.

Instead of diminishing McCarthy's stature, however, the charges had the opposite effect. Republicans in the

The Real Joe McCarthy

Senator Joseph R. McCarthy (right) and Chief Counsel Roy Cohn at the opening of a Senate Investigation Committee session.

Joseph McCarthy grew up as a poor Irish kid from the wrong side of the tracks in Appleton, Wisconsin. A former marine, he boasted that he was a back-alley fighter who had made it to the Senate. But McCarthy was a demagogue and full-fledged alcoholic. He would gulp down a full glass of straight Scotch in one swallow and follow it with another glass of bicarbonate of soda. When drinking heavily, the senator would eat a quarter-pound stick of butter, which he claimed helped him hold his liquor. As quoted by David Halberstam in *The Fifties,* one old friend said McCarthy was "the town drunk in businessman's clothes."

of the Senate in 1952, Senator McCarthy was rewarded with his own permanent investigation committee.

McCarthy never proved that a single person was really a communist, but he made headlines with his wild accusations. For five years, McCarthy's lies and slander ruined the lives of all they touched. McCarthy indulged a personal vendetta against Hollywood and claimed that more than two thousand actors, writers, directors, and producers were communists. As institutes of higher learning, over six hundred college professors were fired because of McCarthyism. Public libraries were forced to remove books by or about communists, socialists, liberals, and even African Americans. Politicians from local city council to the Senate were scrutinized.

To be labeled a communist by McCarthy was tantamount to being called a traitor to one's country. At the time, it was one of the most ruinous of charges. People who were snared in McCarthy's web lost their jobs and their friends. Careers were ruined, marriages were destroyed, and families were torn apart.

Democratic-controlled Senate were disgusted. They claimed the report was another liberal attempt to protect communist traitors. McCarthy emerged stronger and even nastier. When the Republicans took control

COMMUNIST PARTY ORGANIZATION U.S.A-FEB. 9,1950

Joseph McCarthy testifies on communist activities in the United States. McCarthy's allegations against officials in the military, government, movie industry, and other occupations eventually led to his discrediting.

McCarthy understood the theatrics of his hearings. He knew how to dramatically brush aside the protests of his witnesses and how to humiliate frightened, vulnerable people. In the end he produced little besides headlines and fear. He was skilled at making charges in small towns where the local Associated Press writer would pick up the story whether it was truthful or not. McCarthy kept abreast of reporters' deadlines, knowing it was then that they had the least amount of time to check facts. After hearings, McCarthy would invite favored reporters to a reception/press conference where there was plenty of free whiskey and food. If they needed a story, he was willing to invent a charge or two.

Some reporters, however, found McCarthy's tactics repugnant. Reporter George Reedy, who worked for the United Press International (UPI), found covering McCarthy so odious that he quit journalism altogether. "Joe couldn't find a Com-munist in Red Square [Moscow]," said Reedy. "He didn't know Karl Marx from Groucho Marx—but he was a United States Senator." [17]

McCarthy's Censure

McCarthy's fall began when an opponent much stronger than himself—the U.S. Army—took him on. McCarthy had a young personal assistant, G. David Schine, who was a private in the army. Secretary of the Army Robert Stevens charged that McCarthy waged a persistent and tireless campaign to get special treatment of David Schine on ninety separate occasions.

In the summer of 1954, the Senate launched a thirty-five-day investigation of the army's allegations against McCarthy. During the first-ever televised senate hearings, millions of Americans saw McCarthy in action for the first time. When he attacked and slandered respected military officers, his popularity rapidly declined.

McCarthy lashed out at an elderly army lawyer named Joseph Welch, who broke down and wept under the senator's merciless questioning. McCarthy said of the National Lawyer's Guild, of which Welch was a member:

> I don't think you can find anyplace, anywhere, an organization which had done more to defend Communists . . . to defend espionage agents, and to aid the Communist cause.

Welch paled and seemed to have trouble speaking. "Until this moment, Senator," he said, "I think I never really gauged your cruelty and recklessness. You have done enough. Have you no sense of decency?" [18]

Spectators in the packed courtroom cheered. When Americans saw this spectacle in their living rooms, McCarthy's red-baiting career was over. The Senate soon began an investigation into McCarthy's conduct as a senator, which resulted in official censure. Although he remained a senator, after the censure McCarthy was a broken man. He died in 1957.

Although McCarthy's personal reign of terror was over, anticommunist hysteria continued throughout the fifties. In the House of Representatives, years before McCarthy, the House Un-American Activities Committee (HUAC) hunted reds. HUAC continued its activities well into the sixties. Other organizations, including the CIA, were actively involved in red hunting.

Atomic America

The Red scare enhanced the fear of nuclear war among Americans. To calm these fears, the government created the federal Civil Defense Administration (CDA) in 1951. Many of the materials produced by the CDA were intended to prepare schoolchildren for nuclear war—to "alert, not alarm them." [19] Teachers and parents were urged not to become emotional

Subversive Organizations

Eisenhower and the Republicans won the 1952 election by promising to rid American life of communists. Eisenhower's attorney general, Herbert Brownell, published a list of "subversive" organizations. People belonging to these organizations could automatically lose their jobs, especially if they were professors or government workers. The Associated Press picked up the story and published the list in newspapers across the country. It was reprinted in the 1995 book, *Twentieth Century America,* vol. 5, *The Eisenhower Years: 1952–1960.* Below is a shortened version of that list, which demonstrates how people belonging to arts, minorities, or immigrant organizations were branded as subversive. Some of the 192 organizations designated as subversive on July 21, 1953, were:

American Poles for Peace
Chopin Cultural Center
Council of Greek Americans
Council for Jobs, Relief, and Housing
Jewish Cultural Society
National Committee for Freedom of the Press
Russian American Society
United Committee of Jewish Societies
Washington Committee to Defend the Bill of Rights
American Lithuanian Workers' Literary Association
American Women for Peace
Committee for the Negro in the Arts
National Negro Labor Council
Slavic Council of Southern California
Yugoslav Seamen's Club
American Polish League
Frederick Douglass Education Center
Harlem Trade Union Council
Labor Council for Negro Rights
National Labor Council for Peace
People's Drama, Inc.
Puerto Ricans United
Tri-State Negro Trade Union Council
Union of New York Veterans

Bert the Turtle and Atomic Songs

The federal Civil Defense Administration circulated a comic book and a cartoon film that featured Bert the Turtle. To survive nuclear attack, Bert's message was "duck and cover." The movie *Atomic Café* contains ninety minutes of bomb footage, '50s newsreels, government propaganda, and American atomic culture. It shows dozens of army training films and civil defense films that tried to minimize the actual destruction of nuclear weapons, including the *Bert the Turtle* cartoon. The "Bert the Turtle Song" went like this:

> There was a turtle by the name of Bert
> And Bert the Turtle was very alert
> When danger threatened he knew just what to do
> He ducked! And covered! Ducked! And covered!

The narrator went on to speak:

> Now you and I don't have shells to crawl into like Bert the Turtle, we have to cover up in our own way. Now Paul and Patty know this. No matter where they go or what they do they always try to remember what to do if an atom bomb explodes right then. It's a bomb! Duck! And cover! Here's Tony going to his Cub Scout meeting. Tony knows a bomb could explode any time of the year day or night. There's a bomb! Duck! And cover! Sundays, vacation days, holidays, we all must be ready any time if the atomic bomb explodes. It's a bomb! Duck! And cover!

when discussing a possible Soviet nuclear attack. The national PTA urged a "positive mental health program" [20] to ease atomic anxiety. The worst effects of the bomb, such as traumatic injury, shock, burns, radiation sickness, and death were to be played down.

Throughout the 1950s, thousands of American cities staged regular air-raid drills. In New York City alone, civil defense officials tested all 741 air-raid sirens every month. A one-minute alert was followed by a warbling sound that meant "take cover." Schoolchildren conducted "duck and cover" drills: When the teacher yelled "drop" children would crawl under their desks and cover their heads with their hands. Although the premise is ridiculous today, people were taught that they would be protected from the debris generated by a ten-megaton bomb burning hot as the sun if they ducked and covered their heads.

Many school districts distributed student identification tags modeled on military dog tags. The tags were designed to help civil defense workers identify lost or dead children. By 1952, New York City had issued 2.5 million free

Children use the duck-and-cover maneuver atomic attack drill in their elementary classroom during the 1950s.

tags to pupils in public, parochial, and private schools.

Civil defense plans were originally designed for attack with relatively "small" A-bombs. The development of the hydrogen bomb, which could incinerate entire cities, rendered all previous civil defense plans obsolete. Building thousands of bomb-proof bunkers throughout the country was deemed too expensive by the Eisenhower administration. Instead

plans were made to evacuate cities on the basis of a four-to-six-hour warning of a bomb attack.

Learning to Love the Bomb

Nuclear bombs were a fact of life in the fifties. With a power so raw and destructive, the American mind had to be reshaped to weaken moral convictions against wielding such weapons. To that end, the government and the press had to render the bomb harm-

Bomb Shelters

Though the average family could not afford a personal bomb shelter, the federal government was willing to build shelters for a chosen few. According to Susan Jonas and Marilyn Nissenson in *Going, Going, Gone*:

> A secret concrete-and-steel bunker for members of Congress was built in 1958 into a hill adjacent to the luxurious Greenbrier resort in White Sulphur Springs, West VIrginia, 250 miles southwest of Washington. The government also built quarters at Mount Weather in Virginia, where the president, members of the Supreme Court, and other top officials could ride out the emergency.

The government recommended that average citizens dig fallout shelters or prepare them in their basements. *Life* magazine proclaimed the fiction that ninety-seven out of one hundred people would survive if they were in a shelter and offered a section on how to build one:

Two boys emerge from a bomb shelter built in the backyard of their home. Fear of nuclear attack was so prevalent in the 1950s that many private citizens built and provisioned such shelters.

Families could wall off a section of their cellar, sink a reinforced concrete underground bunker in the backyard, or build a double walled bunker aboveground. There were serious debates whether or not the head of a household had the right to gun down any outsider who tried to get into the family shelter. As time passed, speculation centered on the horrors of nuclear winter, subfreezing temperatures, darkness at noon, worldwide fallout, and destruction of the ozone layer. A writer said "there is no hole big enough to hide all of nature in." Civil defense ceased to be a viable solution. No one wanted to live in a devastated and radioactive world.

less, and even lovable. Douglas T. Miller and Marion Nowak detail some of the contorted language so employed in their book *The Fifties: The Way We Really Were:*

> Nuclear bombs were depicted as casual, even friendly. Nuclear euphemisms sprang up: the "sunshine unit" as a measure of Strontium-90 [radiation] levels. Small nuclear bombs were dubbed "kitten bombs." The phenomenon of human bodies being tossed around by blast effects was referred to as "translation" or "displacement." The H-bomb was originally publicized as a "humanitarian bomb," though this was so obviously ludicrous that its permanent nickname became the "clean" bomb. The *New York Times* travel section even ran one feature called "Watching the Bombs Go Off."

The official attitude struck a popular chord. Often the effort was simply associated with small business. A Salt Lake City fast-food stand advertised a "tasty uranium burger, 45¢," and a uranium sundae.[21]

As time passed, Americans became more comfortable with the concepts of mutually assured destruction and explosions by the megaton. After all, most of them were getting by pretty well, and their lives were focused on their growing families. So it might have been with some trepidation that they listened to President Eisenhower's farewell speech in early 1960:

> An immense military establishment and a large arms industry is new in the American experience . . . . We must never let the weight of this combination endanger our liberties or democratic processes. We should take nothing for granted. [22]

The assertion that the military industrial complex could be more dangerous than communism might have given some Americans pause. But another problem would take precedence for many people in the United States, and it wasn't global in scale. It was right at home in cities, towns, and villages in the American South.

Chapter Three

Parents and children who brought a class-action suit known as Brown v. Board of Education *gather on the steps of Virginia's state capitol building. As a result of the suit, the government forcibly integrated America's schools.*

The Struggle for Equality

Millions of white veterans returning home from World War II were offered good jobs in a burgeoning economy. When African American soldiers returned, they faced the same racism and discrimination that had oppressed them before the war. World War II had been fought against the Nazi principle of white (Aryan) superiority over the entire human race. But young black American soldiers who fought the Nazis were segregated in the army and treated as inferiors. Ironically, they found themselves with fewer privileges than the German prisoners of war they might have been guarding.

But things were changing in America, if slowly. During the forties, President Roosevelt signed the Fair

Employment Act, to fight discrimination against African Americans in the job market. In 1944 the National Association for the Advancement of Colored People (NAACP) won a long court fight to ban white-only election primaries. (This decision allowed black people to vote in South Carolina primaries for the first time since 1877.) In 1948, Truman desegregated the military and Supreme Court decisions desegregated graduate schools in the South.

Still, the life of the average African American was not changed by these advances. When columnist Walter Winchell asked a young black woman in Harlem how Hitler should be punished for his crimes, she replied, "Paint him black and send him over here." [23]

African Americans had been living under a policy known as "separate but equal" since 1896, when the Supreme Court ruled that black people could be segregated from whites in schools and virtually all other public facilities as long as they were provided facilities equal in quality. Thereafter, segregation was widely practiced, but equality never came. In the South, states spent an average of ten times more money on schools for whites than they spent on black schools. Most

A sign at a Mississippi bus station points the way to the waiting room for blacks. Such signs were prevalent throughout the South.

black schools were in run-down buildings with few books or supplies.

The South and Jim Crow Laws

The laws that enforced black segregation got their name from a practice of the early 1800s. Black actors were not allowed to perform in theaters attended by whites. Instead, white actors performed in blackface makeup. In 1831 a white singer painted his face black and sang a song called "Jump, Jim Crow." That song quickly became associated with segregation.

By the 1950s, the laws that prohibited African Americans from using white streetcars, restrooms, schools, parks, restaurants, and water foun-

The Soviet View of American Racism

In the war of words between the super-powers, American racism became a potent weapon for the other side. "How could a country that preached freedom and democracy to the rest of the world," the Soviets asked, "condone racism at home?" In *The Fifties: The Way We Really Were*, by Douglas Miller and Marion Nowak, this issue is addressed:

> The Soviet diplomats began to use America's racism as a diplomatic device, to embarrass. This, after all, was a world where whites were a mere minority. The American consensus vision, moreover, demanded complete praise for American ideals and seemed to describe a country of freedom and hope. Racism was unflattering to these facades. It had to be officially decried. As one of Truman's attorney generals said, it "[segregation] furnishes grist for the Communist propaganda mills, and it raises doubts even among friendly nations as to the intensity of our devotion to the democratic faith."

All these practical, face-saving considerations had prompted the forties legal breakthroughs. Genuine moral indignation, or the desire to right stupendous wrongs, seemed to have little to do with it. But at least these justifications proffered a dim recognition that racism did exist, and that it was somehow not very nice.

tains were called Jim Crow laws. They were generally enforced in the American South. African American poet Langston Hughes wrote, "Blacks who wanted to serve their country did so at the risk of their dignity and sometimes at the risk of their lives, long before they met the official enemy. The enemy that hurt them worst was Jim Crow. Jim Crow ignored their citizenship and scorned them as human beings." [24]

On May 17, 1954, in the case of *Brown v. Board of Education of Topeka, Kansas*, the Supreme Court ruled that the "separate but equal" doctrine was unconstitutional. The Court's decision asserted that separate schools were inherently unequal, no matter how they were designed. The landmark ruling stated: "To separate the Negro children from others of a similar age and qualifications solely because of their race generates a feeling of inferiority as to their status in the community that may affect their hearts and minds in a way unlikely ever to be undone." [25]

Two weeks later, the Court ordered all seventeen states with "separate but equal" schools to integrate them immediately. In 1955 the Court extended the ruling to tax-supported colleges and universities.

In this 1954 photograph, two schoolchildren stare at each other after the integration of their elementary school in Virginia.

Brown v. Board of Education sparked social unrest unmatched since the Civil War. The governors of South Carolina, Georgia, and Mississippi threatened to abolish public schools before they would let blacks and whites attend classes together. One hundred senators and congressmen from the South signed a petition against the ruling. Racist hate groups formed to protest the decision. State, county, and city politicians drew up laws to circumvent the Supreme Court ruling. African Americans were once again shown that noble words on paper could not change the reality of the discrimination they faced daily.

Early in 1957, the Eisenhower administration sent Congress a civil rights bill, the first of its kind in the twentieth century. In its original form, the measure provided for a civil rights commission to investigate abuses against black people and permitted the Department of Justice to intervene on behalf of those whose right to vote was denied in southern states. The bill passed the House of Representatives, but in the Senate, it was blocked by the staunch opposition of powerful southern senators.

In protest of the bill, Senator Strom Thurmond of South Carolina filibustered Congress for a record-

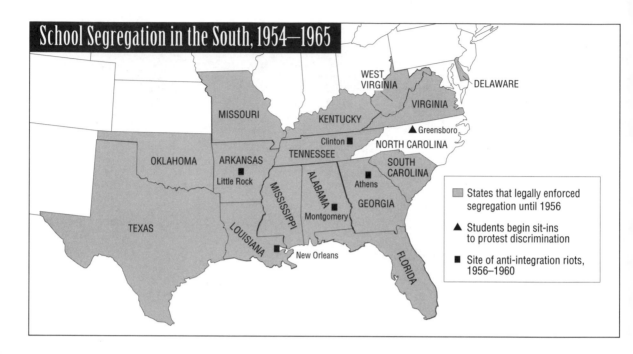

School Segregation in the South, 1954–1965

Map labels: WEST VIRGINIA · DELAWARE · VIRGINIA · MISSOURI · KENTUCKY · ▲ Greensboro · Clinton ■ · NORTH CAROLINA · OKLAHOMA · ARKANSAS · TENNESSEE · SOUTH CAROLINA · Little Rock ■ · MISSISSIPPI · ALABAMA · Athens ■ · GEORGIA · TEXAS · Montgomery ■ · LOUISIANA · New Orleans ■ · FLORIDA

Legend:
- States that legally enforced segregation until 1956
- ▲ Students begin sit-ins to protest discrimination
- ■ Site of anti-integration riots, 1956–1960

breaking twenty-four hours and nineteen minutes. Nevertheless, the bill was finally passed in amended form. Weakened, the measure was mostly symbolic, because it left the civil rights commission powerless and reduced the ability of the federal government to support black voting rights.

White Supremacist Organizations

As guarantees of equal rights for African Americans gained support at the federal level, hate groups organized in opposition. The Ku Klux Klan was formed after the Civil War to keep blacks from benefiting from the abolition of slavery. After a sharp decline in the late 1800s, the KKK enjoyed a revival in the 1920s and again in the 1950s. Members hid their identity behind white sheets, burned crosses as a show of resistance, and resorted to violence when other forms of intimidation failed.

Klansmen were typically rural, undereducated southern white men. Klan units were active from North Carolina to Texas and as far north as Indiana. Members were often unemployed or underemployed outcasts who feared blacks would take their blue-collar and agricultural jobs. The racist doctrine of the Klan also claimed to defend Christianity, the white race, and white women. Members of the Klan were implicated in the bombing of integrated YMCAs, churches, and synagogues.

In 1957 several Klan members in Birmingham, Alabama, kidnapped and tortured a young black man as an initiation rite. They expected the man to die, but he lived to testify against his attackers, each of whom was sentenced to twenty-five years in prison. The Klan suffered other setbacks when they were thoroughly infiltrated by the FBI. (Some Klan chapters had more FBI informants than actual members.)

The Klan came to symbolize racism in the South. But other, less overtly violent organizations called White Citizens' Councils fought integration (and incidentally, rock 'n' roll music) as well, primarily through discriminatory state and local legislation.

Citizens' councils were often made up of the most "respectable" people in the community, including law enforcement officers. Their main weapon was economic power. For example, a local newspaper in Yazoo, Mississippi, ran an ad that printed the names, address-

Ku Klux Klan members of all ages gather at a rally in Macon, Georgia, in 1956. The Klan revived its activities as blacks gained ground in the courts.

es, and phone numbers of blacks who had signed a petition asking local school boards to integrate the schools. The blacks who held jobs lost them.

Fourteen-year-old Emmett Louis Till was kidnapped and slain after talking to a white woman. The murder galvanized blacks and received national media attention.

Local banks cut off their credit. Fifty-one of the fifty-three people who originally signed the petition removed their names. Still, they did not get their jobs back. Similar incidents were commonplace in other small southern towns.

In many places, the white response to ordered integration was open unorganized violence. In Belzoni, Mississippi, whites threatened to shoot any black person who tried to integrate the school. Several black men who tried to vote were later found shot to death along the highway; the sheriff refused to investigate the case. Few of these crimes were covered by the national press. It seemed the backwoods law of Mississippi was more powerful than the new laws handed down from Washington.

The Death of Emmett Till

The national news media largely ignored local violence in the Deep South, but the murder of a young man from Chicago finally galvanized the national press and drew nationwide public reaction. In the summer of 1955, Emmett Till, a fourteen-year-old African American from Chicago, traveled to Tallahatchie County, Mississippi, to visit his mother's family. Till's mother, a Mississippi native, warned Emmitt that the customs of the South were radically different than those of urban Chicago.

Till was a teenager, but at 160 pounds possessed the build of a grown man. He was a sharp dresser and a little bit sassy. These were not crimes in Chicago, but in the oddly named town of Money, Mississippi (one of the poorest towns in America), these qualities could get a black teenager in trouble. On August 25, 1955, Till and his cousin drove to a little grocery store that sold fatback, snuff, and canned goods. The store, patronized almost exclusively by poor rural blacks, was run by Carolyn Bryant, a married, twenty-one-year-old white woman, "a pretty high-school dropout called 'A crossroads Marilyn Monroe' by the French newspaper *Aurore*." [26]

Till and friends passed the time outside the store. At one point Till pulled a photo of a white woman out of his pocket and said she was his girlfriend. One of the disbelieving boys said if Till was so good with white women, why didn't he go into the store and talk to Carolyn Bryant? What happened next is still a matter of some debate. According to some, Till wolf-whistled at Bryant. Others say he went inside and bought two cents worth of bubble gum. As he left, he grabbed her wrist and suggested that they get together. According to Mrs. Bryant's trial testimony, "He grabbed my wrist and then made a lewd suggestion. 'Don't be afraid of me baby. I been with white girls before.'" [27]

Whatever the case, Till quickly left. Carolyn Bryant later told her hus-band, Roy, what had happened. Soon the entire county was buzzing with rumors, gossip, and news about Emmett Till. Unwittingly, Till had violated a deadly serious code of the Deep South. However innocent the slight, Roy Bryant was obliged to defend his wife's honor or lose face in a racist society.

Bryant went looking for Till with his half-brother J. W. Milam, a 235-pound, highly decorated World War II hero. According to a local lawyer, Milam, whose nickname was "Big," "bootlegged all his life. He comes from a big, mean, overbearing family. Got a chip on his shoulder. That's how he got that battlefield promotion in Europe. He likes to kill folks. But hell," the lawyer continued, "we've got to have our Milams to fight our wars and keep the niggahs in line." [28]

Milam and Bryant found Till in the middle of the night. Milam later told a reporter what happened next, as David Halberstam relates in *The Fifties*:

"You the nigger who did the talking?" Milam asked. "Yeah," Till answered. "Don't say 'Yeah' to me: I'll blow your head off." Then they drove away with Till. They did not intend to kill Till, they only wanted to scare him and teach him a lesson. But when he proved unrepentant, only then, much to their sorrow, did they realize they had to kill him. "What else could we do?" Milam explained. "He was hopeless. I'm no bully; I never hurt a nigger in my life. I like niggers in their place. I know how to work on 'em. But I just decided it was time to put a few people on notice. As long as I live and can do anything about it, niggers are going to stay in their place. When a nigger even gets close to mention sex with a white woman, he's tired of livin'. 'Chicago boy,' I said. 'I'm tired of 'em sending your kind down here to stir up trouble. I'm going to make an example of you —so everybody can know how me and my folks stand.'" [29]

Milam and Bryant killed Emmett Till with a .45, crushed his skull in with an ax, tied a 150-pound machine fan around his neck for weight, stripped him naked, and threw him in the Tallahatchie River. When a reporter later asked Milam if he had been nervous, Milam said, "Yeah, somebody might see us and accuse us of stealing the fan." [30]

Till's badly mangled, waterlogged body was found three days later and returned to Chicago, where ten thousand people stood in line at Till's funeral to view the body in an open casket. The governor of Mississippi called for a complete investigation. Milam and Bryant were arrested for kidnapping and later indicted on murder charges.

The murder electrified the black community and white newspapers finally began to pay attention. Young reporters swarmed into the South to find they were scorned by the local whites. The mur-

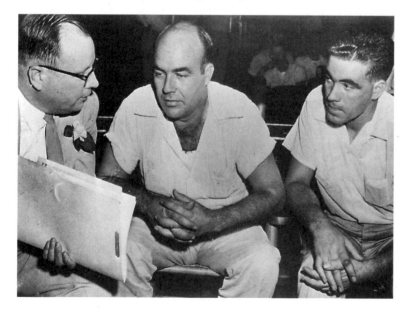

J. W. Milam (center) and Roy Bryant (right) confer with their lawyer after their indictment for the murder of Emmett Till.

der of Emmett Till and the trial of the two men who murdered him became the first big media event of the civil rights movement.

The trial proceeded in typical southern fashion. The county sheriff claimed that Till was not dead but whisked out of the county by the NAACP to make whites look bad. A black congressman from Detroit who attended the trial was referred to by deputies as "a nigger congressman." There was no difficulty raising a defense fund for the defendants.

Everyone knew Milam and Bryant would go free. As the trial wore on they were seen picnicking with their families on the courthouse steps. African Americans who had witnessed the kidnapping were afraid to testify for fear of their lives. The jury deliberated for one hour before setting Bryant and Milam free. "It would have been a quicker decision," said the jury foreman, "if we didn't stop to drink a bottle of pop." [31]

But despite the acquittal, something had changed: Bryant and Milam's white neighbors turned on them. The banks refused to lend them

The Great Black Migration

After the murder of Emmett Till, dozens of the African Americans in Money, Mississippi, boarded trains and moved north. They joined millions of other blacks who were part of the greatest migration in American history. David Halberstam describes the phenomenon in his book *The Fifties*:

At train and bus stations every day, large families of poor blacks clustered, often two or three generations huddling together. They were dressed in their best but their poverty was plainly visible. They carried everything they owned, lugging their belongings in cardboard suitcases or wrapped in bundles of old newspapers tied together by string; they carried food in shoe boxes. They went north largely without possessions and yet they left behind almost nothing.

They were going to Chicago, Detroit, Toledo, and Cleveland, where the work force had previously been made up of Slavs and Germans and Italians. But when the supply of European immigrants dried up, America's great employers [carmakers, steel mills, and factories] turned quickly to the blacks in the South. So they went: first a few adventurous individuals, then whole families, church groups, sometimes it seemed, whole towns.

money. Their little store was boycotted by blacks and soon closed. They were told, in effect, to get out of town.

Rosa Parks Sparks a Bus Boycott

The murder of Emmett Till was making headlines. But life went on in the South as it had for decades. Montgomery, Alabama, for example, was a typical town in southern America. About 48,000 of its 120,000 residents were African American. Montgomery whites earned an average of $2,000 a year, blacks only $970. Most blacks lived in dilapidated housing, often without running water or electricity, on streets that the city refused to clean or pave. A city ordinance made it illegal for blacks and whites to play cards or checkers together.

Whites owned nearly all of the automobiles in town; blacks depended on city buses for transportation. To board the bus, blacks had to pay their fare up front, get off the bus, and reenter through the back door. Sometimes a bus driver would roar off as the rider was walking around to the back door.

There were hundreds of towns like Montgomery in the South. But a group of dedicated African Americans put the racist struggles in Montgomery onto the headlines of newspapers throughout the world.

On the evening of December 1, 1955, a neatly dressed, black woman named Rosa Parks left her place of employment at quitting time. She walked across the street to do some shopping, then boarded a Montgomery city bus for the ride home. Parks walked to the back of the bus and took a seat just behind the section marked "Whites Only." After a long day as a tailor's assistant, her feet, neck, and shoulders hurt. She was glad to sit down with her packages. As the bus wound its way through town, it filled with passengers until every seat in the "Whites Only" section was taken. Two more white men boarded the bus. The driver yelled over his shoulder for the first two rows of blacks to move back.

After a few minutes, three black people rose and stood in the aisle. Rosa Parks, her lap covered with packages and her feet aching, refused to move. The driver shouted at her to get up. Parks would not budge. The police were called and Parks was arrested and thrown in jail. Parks was desperately thirsty in jail, but police would not let her use the water fountain because it too was marked "Whites Only."

Rosa Parks had violated a law that stated not only that blacks sit at the back of the bus in a separate section, but that they surrender their seats to whites if the buses were full. This policy was enforced in Montgomery even though there were forty thousand black bus riders and only twelve thousand white riders.

The NAACP and its former leader, Edgar Daniel Nixon, had been searching for years for a way to fight bus discrimination in Montgomery. When Rosa Parks was arrested, Nixon called nineteen black ministers in Montgomery to help organize a bus boycott. More than thirty-five thousand flyers were printed and distributed by students and other volunteers. The flyers explained why Rosa Parks had been arrested and asked every black person to stay off the city buses for one day, Monday, December 5, the day Parks was to go on trial. The flyers were circulated secretly in light of the very real risk of job loss, injury, and even lynching.

On Monday the buses were empty. Montgomery's eighteen black-owned taxi companies agreed to transport people for the same fare as

Rosa Parks is fingerprinted after her arrest for refusing to give a white man her seat on a public bus in Montgomery, Alabama. Blacks protested the arrest by boycotting the buses.

the bus—ten cents. That night, thousands of people gathered in churches to rally against segregation and Jim Crow. A new minister in town, the twenty-six-year-old Dr. Martin Luther King Jr., gave a fiery speech to thousands of boycotters from his pulpit. Hundreds more listened through loudspeakers out on the street. It was decided that night that the boycott

The Reverends Martin Luther King Jr. (right) and Ralph Abernathy (center) stand as King is booked for assisting with the bus boycott in Montgomery, Alabama.

would last until segregation was ended. For thirteen months, empty buses rolled through the streets of Montgomery.

Montgomery's white citizens were unsympathetic to blacks' demands. On January 30, King's house was fire-bombed while his wife, Coretta, hid in a back room with their seven-month-old baby in her arms. On February 1, Nixon's house was firebombed. Later, King and twenty-four others were arrested under an antiquated law barring boycotts.

Throughout the boycott, King continued to preach a message of non-violence:

If we are arrested every day, if we are exploited every day, if we are trampled down every day, let nobody pull you so low as to hate them. We must use the weapon of love. We must have compassion and understanding for those who hate us. So many people have been taught to hate, taught from the cradle. They are not totally responsible. [32]

On December 20, 1956, the Supreme Court struck down the Montgomery bus laws. Martin Luther King continued to preach against segregation and organize boycotts across the South.

Black and White in Little Rock

By the late summer of 1957 the process of school integration had reached Little Rock, Arkansas. A federal court ordered the previously all-white Central High School to admit black students. The battle had begun two years earlier when Daisy Bates, a black newspaper publisher, organized a campaign to enroll nine students at Central High. Her windows were broken by a rock-throwing mob, her house was sprayed with bullets, and crosses were burned on her lawn. Forty-four teachers who favored integration were fired.

On September 5, 1957, nine students were poised to begin school at Central High. The governor of Arkansas, Orval Faubus, posted Arkansas National Guardsmen in front of the school

Racism in the Nation's Capitol

Frederic Morrow was the first black special assistant to work in the White House. He was a rarity in the 1950s, a black Republican. In 1952 he was asked to be a liaison between the black community and the campaign of Dwight Eisenhower. After accepting the job, Morrow was subjected to an endless array of humiliation. David Halberstam writes about Morrow's troubles in *The Fifties*:

> After Ike was elected, Morrow believed he had been given a job in the White House . . . and moved [from New York City] to Washington. He was stunned by what he found there. White cab drivers would not pick up a black man. Blacks could not eat in white restaurants or stay in white hotels. There was virtually no integrated housing. Even when the resources of the White House were summoned on his behalf, little turned up. Finally it was decided to pressure the owner of a big residential hotel, who was said to be a major contributor to the Eisenhower campaign. The owner said yes, he would offer Morrow an apartment but Morrow would have to use the freight elevator to get to his room and he could not use the main lobby, nor could he eat in the building's restaurant. I am supposed to work in the White House, for the President of the United States, and I can barely find a place to live and eat, Morrow thought.

Whites protest against the integration of Little Rock Junior High School in Arkansas. Blacks had to fight to integrate schools, even though they were legally granted the right to attend them.

to keep the black students out. White mobs gathered and threatened violence. No black students entered school that day.

For weeks, a battle raged in several courtrooms. Eisenhower met with Faubus and ordered him to open Central High to blacks. Faubus refused. On September 23, the Little Rock Nine, as they were now called, tried to go to school again. Police cars arrived carrying the students, who slipped past the mobs into the side door of the school. Three hundred white students ran out the front entrance. When the mob realized what had happened, they vented

their anger on white reporters who were covering the event. Journalists and photographers from national magazines were beaten and their cameras were destroyed. The mob screamed, cursed, and wept as the black students looked out from the school windows.

That evening, Eisenhower ordered troops of the 101st Airborne Division to Little Rock. He went on national television to explain his decision to send federal troops to maintain order. The next morning, 350 paratroopers stood in front of Central High. Soldiers in jeeps mounted with machine guns escorted the students to

Black students from Central High School in Little Rock receive an escort from two paratroop officers in 1957. It eventually took federal troops to integrate the school.

school. Helicopters circled overhead. Once inside, each student was assigned a bodyguard and classes resumed. At the end of the day the students were taken home under guard.

Inside the school, a few white students befriended the Little Rock Nine. Several whites went on record to defend the black students' right to an equal education. But for the rest of the year, the Little Rock Nine endured name-calling, shoving, and tripping.

Meanwhile, Americans saw scared, innocent black children carrying their books and lunches to school on the daily news. Behind armed soldiers, white adults shouted horrible

obscenities at them. The troops stayed in Little Rock until Thanksgiving, two days after Ike suffered a stroke that left him temporarily unable to speak.

Orval Faubus thwarted the Supreme Court orders by shutting Little Rock's public schools completely. White students attended private schools. Blacks had no school to attend. The battle went on until 1962, when Little Rock finally integrated its schools.

African American struggles for equality continued well into the 1960s. But the fight for freedom seemed remote to most middle-class Americans living in suburbs far outside the troubled South.

Chapter Four

Children play on a swing set during the 1950s in one of the new suburban developments.

Growing Up in the Fifties

The fifties may have been marred by racism and the threat of nuclear annihilation, but many Americans floated through those years on a cloud of prosperity and family values. An emphasis on marriage, children, and family life prevailed throughout the decade. The thirties had been the era of the Great Depression, when couples could not afford children and lived in crowded shacks, flats, or dilapidated apartments. The forties were war years, when women worked while husbands, fathers, brothers, and boyfriends marched off to battle. Many returned with serious injuries; some never returned at all. By the fifties, Americans had had enough of deprivation and anguish.

Men and women of the 1950s married at an early age—on average, twenty-two for men and nineteen for women. The divorce rate, which had risen slowly from the 1920s, leveled off at 10 percent. Divorce was stigmatized and considered socially unacceptable.

Before the fifties, due to housing shortages and economic hard times, children usually grew up in a house shared by their grandparents, aunts, uncles, and other extended family members. But in the fifties, suburban "nuclear families" were comprised only a mother, father, and children. Middle-class family activities emphasized togetherness—families went to church, went on vacation, saw ball games, worked in the yard, watched television, and washed the car. And they multiplied: Between 1946 and 1964, 30 million children were born—more than 4 million a year after the mid-1950s. This "baby boom" formed a huge demographic category that influenced everything from the sale of diapers and cars to the popularity of rock 'n' roll.

Identical tract homes line the streets of this suburban neighborhood of the 1950s. Such homes were built in mass quantities to house the families that gave birth to the baby-boom generation.

William Levitt Invents the Suburbs

After World War II, the housing shortage reached crisis proportions. It was so bad in Chicago that 250 used trolley cars were sold as homes. William J. Levitt began to solve this problem when he began mass-producing seventeen thousand new, reasonably priced homes in Hempstead, Long Island, twenty miles from New York City. It was the largest housing project in American history. Douglas T. Miller and Marion Nowak write about Levitt's houses in their book *The Fifties: The Way We Really Were*:

On July 3, 1950, William J. Levitt was pictured on the cover of *Time*. The portrait showed him standing in front of a neat row of identical boxlike houses set up like Monopoly pieces on land newly bulldozed to a uniform flatness. The cover caption read: "HOUSE BUILDER LEVITT: For Sale: a new way of life." Levitt, who called his firm "the General Motors of the housing industry," brought mass-production techniques to house-building. First on Long Island and then outside of Philadelphia, he turned farmlands into giant Levittowns. His houses were unvarying in floorplan with seven color choices and a tree planted every 28 feet (two and a half trees per home). "The best house in the U.S." bragged Levitt of his picture-windowed box complete with a refrigerator, stove, Bendix washer in each kitchen, and an Admiral TV built into every living room. Deeds to Levitt's houses specified that lawns were to be mowed at least once a week in season, and laundry could be hung only on rotary racks, no clotheslines. When one man mounted a gargoyle on his house, it became such a famous sight that residents drove out of their way to show it to visitors. Such was the new suburban utopia.

A Job and a House in the Suburbs

Americans saw the fifties as blessed by progress. The GI Bill, which focused on education and housing, stimulated a huge construction boom fueled by highly educated workers. Many men who had just spent four years in the army got married, went to college, and started a family all at once.

Inexpensive, assembly-line housing sprang up on the East Coast and was soon imitated everywhere. Thousands of very similar houses were crowded into instant suburbs on the outskirts of big cities. Families could have modern appliances, individual bedrooms, garages, and lawns for as little as $6,000 in the late forties. Veterans used low-interest loans to snap up the houses, and the suburban boom was born.

In the fifties, most Americans who lived in the suburbs worked in central cities, and job security and benefits were unprecedented. Labor unions had secured wages sufficient to put skilled workers in the middle class. Huge corporations were paying their white-collar workers very well. People expected to hold one job their entire lives and retire at age sixty-two.

But young executives paid a price for their job security. The often unwritten rules of 1950s corporate life could be quite rigid. For instance, socializing after work was part of the job. And the ability to drink large quantities of liquor without visible effect was expected. One 1956 employment ad that ran in the *New York Times* read:

A businessman conducts a meeting in the 1950s. Business emphasized conformity in the 1950s, and executives were expected to be available at all times to do the company's bidding.

> Salesmgr: Intangible exp, must be able to move effectively at top mgmt level and effectively understand "Big Business" problems. Should be able to handle 12 martinis.[33]

Though the twelve-martini requirement might have been facetious, it does show the reality of the corporate world. By the midfifties American corporations were producing more than

consumer goods; they were shaping lifestyles and values for millions of Americans.

Executives were expected to dress alike, join country clubs, play golf, and return to suburbia and a doting family every night. Since almost all executives were men, women were forced to operate under different, but equally narrow, rules.

Women, called "helpmates," were to look after the children, keep the house spotless, and mingle with other wives at company gatherings. For single adults,

The Cost of Living in the Good Old Days

People fondly remember the fifties as the good old days, when the average house cost $14,500, a haircut was $1.50, and a gallon of gasoline was 30 cents. But a 1998 study by the Federal Reserve Bank showed those things relatively cheaper than they were back then. In 1950 the average wage earner made $1.44 an hour. In 1998 that figure was $13.18 an hour, not including benefits. That means that an average worker worked less hours to pay for standard family items than his or her counterpart did in the fifties.

For example, it took a fifties' worker 1,638 hours to pay for an average-priced $3,030 car. In 1998, that worker worked 1,365 hours—almost three hundred hours less—to pay for an $18,000 car. (And 1998 automobiles were safer, more fuel efficient, less likely to need major repairs, more durable, and more comfortable.) A fifties' worker worked 6.5 hours per square foot of his home.

In 1998 that figure was 5.6 hours per square foot.

The study found similar figures across a whole range of items: A $420 kitchen range required 292 hours of work. In 1998 that average range costs only $299 and requires 23 hours of work. A coast-to-coast airplane flight cost $110 and required 71 hours of work. In 1998 that flight costs about $209 and requires only 16 hours of work. Perhaps the biggest change is in long-distance telephone calls. A brief coast-to-coast call in 1950 set the caller back $2.50 and required 1.5 hours of work to pay for. In 1998 that call costs 90 cents and requires only 4.2 minutes of a worker's wages. In 1950s prices, that same call would cost $19.77. The report did point out however, that some things, such as college tuition and medical care, are considerably more expensive today.

minorities, homosexuals, childless couples, and the elderly, the conformist corporate rules bordered on the repressive.

The Role of Women

In the years before the women's liberation movement, fifties women were simply expected to perform the jobs of stay-at-home mothers. A widely read book, *The Women's Guide to Better Living*, advised, "The family is the unit to which you most genuinely belong. . . .

The family is the center of your living. If it isn't, you've gone far astray." [34]

The prevailing wisdom was that men and women were so different as to be members of separate species. Men were thought to be tough, individualistic, unemotional, solid, and aggressive. A woman's basic need, it was said, was to be wife, mother, and homemaker. Her primary achievement and fulfillment was childbearing. TV personality Alan Ludden noted in one of his advice books that a teenage girl

A 1950s housewife dressed in the garb of her profession. Men's and women's roles were strictly defined in the decade.

"knows that as a woman she will be doing a great deal more for others than will be done for herself." [35] Writer Paul Landis assured women: "Except for the sick, the badly crippled, the deformed, the emotionally warped, and the mentally defective, almost everyone has an opportunity to marry." [36]

Aside from pronouncements in books and magazines, many women with young families simply did not want their own careers. Some women were disenchanted by the rules forced on them but many seemed happy to stay at home. Few women thought about feminism as it is conceived today. The women's movement of the early 1900s was remembered fondly as having won the vote for female adults in 1920. But others continued to blame it for perceived problems such as pacifism, declining religious belief, and even the Great Depression.

Women also served society in many ways. They volunteered for charity drives, as Boy and Girl Scout den mothers, on boards of Parent Teacher Associations, and taught Sunday school.

Bridge Parties

During the 1950s as many as 40 million Americans played bridge. Bridge was the most popular card game and cards were the most popular game. Susan Jonas and Marilyn Nissenson remember America's obsession with bridge in their book *Going, Going, Gone*:

> In the October 13, 1957, *New York Times,* a reporter characterized the social life of middle-class American couples: "The Smiths have the Browns to dinner and then the Browns have the Smiths to dinner. After they eat, they must do something. Television is hardly social; conversation is a lost art; cards are an acceptable solution." So the Smiths and the Browns play a few hands of bridge.
>
> Mrs. Smith and Mrs. Brown also got together with six other housewives from the neighborhood for a Thursday afternoon bridge party. On Mrs. Smith's day to entertain, she set up two folding bridge tables in her living room and laid out her pink linen bridge cloths and napkins. After a lunch of chicken à la king and peas, the "girls," as they call themselves, settle down to play. The winner could clear five dollars at the end of the day. Sometimes the girls put all their winnings into a kitty, which they spent on an annual dinner party for their husbands—"the men."
>
> Mrs. Smith's daughter, Jane, came home from school and was allowed to sit in on a hand or two. When she went off to college, she found several regular foursomes in her dorm. Bridge seemed second only to boys, and way ahead of books, as a topic of interest.

In the 1920s, almost half of all college students were women. By the 1950s, that number had dropped to 35 percent. Many women's colleges closed or became coeducational. Fewer than 20 percent of all science and math majors were women. Careers reflected this educational level. Although 19.3 million women had entered the workforce, the most common jobs by far were low-paying clerical jobs, nursing, and teaching. A few women did pursue careers in medicine, law, and the sciences.

Children in the Fifties

The rigid gender roles of the fifties were also expected of children. Girls played with dolls, especially Barbie. Boys continued to play with toy guns and cars. Both sexes circled the block on their pricey Schwinn bicycles.

Boys hung baseball gloves from their handlebars and wore Levis or Lee jeans. Chinos were worn to school or church. After the *Davy Crockett* show went on the air, many boys wore coonskin caps and frontiersman

Preteens, riding bikes that simulate the car design of the era, gather at the local park. Notice the children's clothing, including the girl's pedal pushers and the boy's cuffed denim jeans.

shirts. Older kids might have affected a rebellious look with engineer's boots, leather coats, T-shirts, and jeans.

Girls played in midcalf pedal pushers and idealized cowgirl Dale Evans. For school, they wore wash-and-wear dresses and blouses made from synthetic materials. Older girls might have tuned in to Dick Clark's *American Bandstand* to see the teenagers dancing to rock music.

In school, progressive education treated children as singular beings rather than imperfect adults. Educators of the day read the works of psychoanalyst Sigmund Freud, who stressed the importance and uniqueness of childhood. From such concepts came the *Common Sense Book of Baby and Child Care,* by Dr. Benjamin Spock. According to the 1997 *Grolier's Multimedia Encyclopedia:*

> *Common Sense Book of Baby and Child Care* was a dramatic contrast to earlier child-care books that had favored rigid feeding schedules and had warned against

Teenage girls sip their sodas. Teens' earning power allowed them to purchase more goods than previous generations.

success. Calmly and confidently, Spock told new parents all the things they might have been taught by a mother or grandmother a generation earlier. Spock's kids enjoyed an informal, commonsense childhood. According to Douglas Miller and Marion Nowak, "Spockian parents feel that it is their responsibility to make their child into the most all-around perfect adult possible. The child has his entire being involved with parental aspirations." [38]

Teenage America

White suburban children of the postwar baby boom were the best fed, best schooled, and best cared-for generation in history—and the richest. As one commentator remarked in the midfifties, "Teen-agers of today are stronger, smarter, more self-sufficient and more constructive than any other generation of teen-agers in history." [39] Youth occupied a favored position in fifties America; teens were seen as unique human beings set apart by a generation gap.

showing a child too much affection. Spock's book was reassuring in its support of maternal tenderness. It answered practical questions not even addressed by earlier works and (even though it was later accused of encouraging "permissiveness") encouraged parents to set standards and expectations for their children. [37]

Spock's book achieved instant

In reality, fifties mass culture was dominated by business, and business expected and encouraged people to indulge in conspicuous consumption. Teens were no exception. In earlier times, when teenagers made money, their earnings went to support their parents or were saved for a treasured item, such as a bicycle, or college. But fifties teenagers, with no memory of the Depression, were not pressured to save money. They became a brand-new consumer class.

Scholastic magazine showed that by 1956 there were 13 million teenagers in the country with a total income of $7 billion a year, a figure 26 percent higher than in 1953. The average teenager had an income of $10.55 a week. This figure represented the disposable income of an entire family in 1940. They spent it on such items as TVs, phonographs, records, pimple cream, and lipstick (alone worth $20 million in 1958).

As newer, bigger, and flashier products filled the marketplace, the value of the new kept rising. Anything old (including people) was seen as old-fashioned, even obsolete. At the same time, parents who lived through the Depression and war wanted to

Fifties Women's Fashions

Women's fashions in the fifties reflected the primness that society expected of females. Waists were tight and often pinched to the point of agony by girdles. Skirts were A-line or full and hemlines reached well below the knee. Permed hair and polka dots were in, along with high heels. Brett Harvey writes about women's clothing in her book *The Fifties: A Women's Oral History*:

> Did you ever think about the fact that all the fabrics we wore in the fifties were *stiff?* Nothing clung, or fell, or draped—everything was crisp. Forties clothes were truly sexy—those swingy little dresses in soft, flowered rayon prints with shoulder pads and a jaunty, competent femininity. Fifties clothes were like armor. Our clothes expressed all the contradictions of our roles. Our ridiculously starched skirts and hobbling sheaths were a caricature of femininity. Our cinched waists and aggressively pointed breasts advertised our availability at the same time they warned of our impregnability.
>
> In the daytime we wore tight, revealing sweaters, but they were topped by mincing little Peter Pan collars and perky scarves that seemed to say, "Who, *me?* Why, I'm just a little girl!" At night, our shoulders were naked, the lower half of our bodies hidden in layers of tulle (a fine net of nylon). Underneath it all our flesh was "contained" by boned girdles, in an era when "containment" was a political as well as a social obsession.

give their children everything they themselves had been denied. New clothes, toys, radios, and even a college education became a right, not a privilege.

Technology also favored the young. Before the 1950s, a typical family owned only one radio and one record player. Parental control could still be exercised over which programs or records were played. But with the invention of the transistor radio, the prices of such appliances rapidly dropped. Radios sold for $25 to $50, record players for $47. Teenagers were asked to put $1 down and pay $1 a week. Phonograph manufacturers sold more than 10 million record players a year, as credit buying reached the young.

Life After High School

The military draft was still a reality for fifties males. Teens who did not go to college, realizing they would be drafted sooner or later, enlisted for three to six years in a branch of the armed forces. There they would receive vocational training and see the world.

Girls who graduated from high school without college plans often felt pressure to get married. They took jobs as clerks and secretaries while they waited for "Mr. Right." Typical starting pay for young adults was about $65 a week. Many continued to live with parents so they could afford nice clothes and a car.

The road to success began with a college education. By the late fifties, over 3.5 million students were enrolled in colleges and universities, which by and large embraced corporate culture. By 1954, more than one in five students were pursuing business degrees. Commercial fields of study grew more specialized. Courses were offered in hotel and restaurant management, packaging, advertising, and even mobile home design, construction, and sales.

Personal attitudes were increasingly geared toward business life. Students fully accepted the status quo and expected to reap ample rewards from their education. Most business students were politically conservative and religious. One student who was a "big man on campus" told *Parade* magazine:

> You have to be very careful not to associate with the wrong clan of people, an introvert that isn't socially acceptable, guys who dress in the fashion of ten years ago, blue serge suits and loud ties. These people are just not accepted—and, if you associate with them, you're not accepted either. [40]

Eighteen-year-olds appear at the selective service station in New York to register for the draft. Teens who did not go to college were guaranteed to be drafted into the armed forces.

A study called *Changing Values in College,* published in 1957, showed that most college students had fully absorbed the values of their times. The survey revealed that 59 percent of students felt that a lot of teachers had radical ideas that should be carefully watched. Forty percent felt the Communist Party should be outlawed and radicals of any sort should be barred from teaching. A majority of students also stated that conscientious objectors (people who refused to fight wars on religious or other grounds) should be expelled from the country.

Of course not every university scholar was eager to accommodate big business. In 1959 a University of Southern California professor wrote in a letter to *Nation* magazine:

"The commercialism and conformity in idea and action by the men who fill our colleges would nauseate the naive." He went on to describe "the bowing and scraping . . . the uniformity of dress, speech, attitudes and behavior; the almost complete suppression of honesty and frankness," on the part of the faculty. [41]

Critics dubbed the youth of the fifties "the Silent Generation." The majority attended mainstream churches or synagogues on a regular basis. When they played they went to sporting events, ate pizza, and danced. Business types intended to vote Republican (the voting age was then twenty-one) because that's what their future corporate bosses did. Frequently the only voice in the classroom questioning practices such as

red-baiting, nuclear fallout, or racism belonged to the instructor.

Summing Up the Fifties Family

Magazine quotes and statistics cannot describe every individual during the fifties. But the era was unique in that so many people experienced the exact same things at the same time: the end of the war, the rise of the suburbs, booming technology, and the centrality of the nuclear family, accompanied by widespread conformity of action and ideas.

Those who lived through those times might not remember them as we do today. But there is a reason we see the decade as we do: We can observe fifties Americans every day living, loving, and laughing when we watch the television programs of the age.

Chapter Five

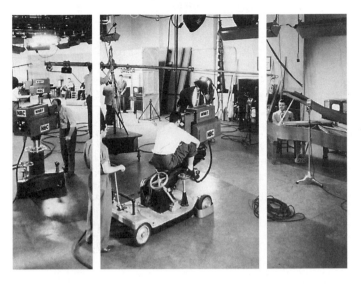

An early television studio films a pianist. Many early television programs were filmed in front of a live audience.

The Golden Age of Television

From exploding H-bombs to the hip-shaking Elvis Presley, Americans watched the images of the fifties flicker by on black-and-white television sets. It was those small-screened televisions in lacquered wooden consoles that permanently changed how Americans saw the world—and how the world saw America.

Before 1945, the medium of TV existed only as a clumsy and expensive toy for the wealthy. But the wartime invention of the Image Orthicon "picture" tube made inexpensive television sets a reality. In 1946 only seven thousand TV sets existed in the United States. By 1950, 4.4 million families were tuning in to the wonders of television. By 1956

Early TV Programs

In the beginning, all television programming consisted of locally produced shows. Because there was no central distributor for these shows, early stations had to improvise, usually with less than exciting results. The positive side was that local performers often got a chance at success on new TV stations. Here, taken from J. Fred MacDonald's *One Nation Under Television*, is a programming schedule from WRGB in Schenectady, New York.

July 16: *Hoe-Down Night,* a musical barn dance with square dancing and instructors to teach viewers how to square dance.

July 23: *A Day at the Circus,* an actual circus with a clown, band, ringmaster, peanut vendor, and performers emanating from the Schenectady studio.

August 6: Experimental commercial shows sponsored by Goodrich Tire consisting of an in-studio demonstration of the making of synthetic rubber plus displays of the new rubber derivative latex.

August 19: An Afro-American religious revival made possible when station personnel convinced the organizers to move their gathering inside the Schenectady studio.

September 9: A stark presentation on blood plasma that includes an actual blood donation made by a WRGB foreman.

October 7: *Bridge on Television* offers two expert card teams and a commentator. The players use oversized cards to make their hands visible to the camera.

November 11: A complete presentation of Shakespeare's *The Taming of the Shrew.*

people were buying TV sets at the rate of twenty thousand *a day.* In 1960, Americans owned 50 million televisions and 90 percent of American homes boasted at least one TV.

Sales of televisions boosted unexpected sales of other items. In 1955 alone, Americans bought 4 million new refrigerators. The reason? Frozen food. Old refrigerators had tiny freezers with room only for a few ice cube trays. New refrigerators were designed for a brand-new invention, TV din-

ners. The family sit-down dinner was replaced by food consumed from aluminum trays in front of the TV.

This remarkable change struck people as only mildly surprising. Television was just one more product that proved American affluence. Owning a television meant both status and entertainment. These simple concepts disguised the astounding changes TV introduced. Television changed the way people looked, acted, and consumed. This common

A housewife pauses in her multiple tasks to watch Joseph McCarthy on television. McCarthy's bullying and obnoxious style was revealed in homes throughout the United States, eventually contributing to his downfall.

invention was the most sudden and dramatic development in communications history.

The early days of TV are often called the golden age of television. Even through the rosy haze of nostalgia, this assessment is true on some levels. The first TV viewers/purchasers were affluent people; programming was designed to appeal to their taste for the arts and performances of high quality. Early broadcasts included opera, live original dramas, recreations of Broadway shows, quality

documentaries, and variety shows along with a range of comedy, news, and adventure. Added to this mix was the fact that most of TV in those days was broadcast live. It was immediate and authentic. Flubbed lines, accidents on the set, and stage fright added to the excitement of the shows.

Live TV also showed millions of people the workings of their government for the first time. This was best demonstrated during the Army-McCarthy hearings broadcast live in 1954 and watched by millions. When

Americans saw the unfair, bullying tactics of Senator McCarthy, his four-year reign of terror ended almost overnight.

Changing Patterns in American Life

Before television, entertainment generally cost money. But once a TV was paid for, the signal was free. This immediately rocked America's entertainment business. In the early fifties, movie attendance fell 40 percent. Movie theaters shut their doors. In

The stars of the popular television series Leave It to Beaver. *Such shows idealized the family and always ended harmoniously.*

New York City in 1951, 55 theaters went out of business. In southern California that number reached 134. People went out less and less in the evening. Spare time was devoted to watching TV.

Almost all other aspects of American life were affected by the television boom. Radio listenership dropped significantly. Book sales went down and libraries complained of diminished activity. People went to restaurants earlier. Sales of products advertised on TV soared. Even city utilities were affected: Studies showed that when a popular show ended, millions of toilets flushed at the same time, as if on cue.

There was a negative side to the new medium. Television functioned best when presenting simple stories in neat thirty-minute units. By the late fifties, TV portrayed an antiseptic world of idealized homes in an unflawed America. Shows like *Leave It to Beaver* and *Ozzie and Harriet* showed families with a working father, a mother who cooked and cleaned, and children who only got into minor mischief. On *Leave It to Beaver*, Ward Cleaver once asked his wife, June, "What type of girl would you have Wally [their older son] marry?" "Oh," answered June. "Some very sensible girl from a nice family . . . one with both feet on the ground, who's a good cook, and can keep a nice house, and see that he's happy." [42]

There were no financial problems, no ethnic tensions, and few if any minority characters. Racial stereotypes were reenforced—southerners, for example, were portrayed as simple rustics in *The Real McCoys*. Blacks were portrayed as stuttering schemers in *The Amos and Andy Show*. Women were portrayed as impeccably dressed helpmates on shows like *Ozzie and Harriet*.

Programming to the Masses

As had already happened in radio, the television industry quickly became dominated by corporations who claimed to know what was best for Americans. Television influenced the masses but the masses could do very little to influence television. Those who controlled the medium gained powers never before imagined. By mid-decade the wide variety of live, quality programming dwindled and was replaced by bland, pretaped, homogenized shows.

At first, television was hailed as a tool of universal communication.

Controlling the Message of TV

Factions within the U.S. government were quick to realize the controlling power of television. During the Red scare of the early fifties, some officials were afraid that the wrong type of programming on TV could corrupt Americans and turn them into communists. Douglas T. Miller and Marion Nowak explain the official reaction to TV in *The Fifties: The Way We Really Were*:

> In 1950, three ex-FBI agents published a book called *Red Channels*. This book, and others like it, affected the young TV industry. It provided both the justification and structure for systematic blacklisting. The logic supporting the lists was one of censorship. Certain people's mere presence was assumed to corrupt the audience. That idea, resounding as it did of authoritarianism, of privileged information, of scorn for public intellect, and of devious control of lives, was typical of early fifties culture. Countless actors, writers, directors, and others lost their livelihood to the blacklists. The censorship and purges became regular practices within the TV industry.

People thought it would provide Americans with a broad education of world events. But the main purpose of television was not to educate but to amuse and sell products. And television was a salesman's dream. In 1949 the advertising industry—based on

William Boyd as Hopalong Cassidy. The popular TV show made millions of dollars in toys and clothing that were based on the show.

Cassidy became so popular that "Hoppy" became a children's idol. Department stores found that Hoppy-related toys sold out in a matter of days. The fad grossed $100 million before it petered out. But it taught a firm lesson: The presence of TV in so many homes provided unheard-of advertising potential.

Thanks to the kiddy cowboy fad, advertisers realized that they needed to appeal to the greatest numbers of people. And, as Miller and Nowak write:

> thanks to the anti-communist purges, they learned oversensitive and simplistic notions of an audience's corruptibility or delicacy. Add to this the ad agencies' realization that sponsors' money paid for TV. Combined, these factors had an unpleasant result. TV became regarded as no more than a commercial medium. The public came to be seen as a childlike herd, easily swayed or spooked, capricious, and by turns greedy and anxious. In the eyes of advertisers and network executives, [Americans] became pliant, eager, and ultimately dehumanized—the audience. [43]

Madison Avenue in New York—billed $12 million for TV ads. The next year, that figure was $40 million, the year after that $128 million.

Executives first realized the commercial potential of television in 1950. A cowboy show called *Hopalong*

The results were predictable. Television became dominated by the big three networks—CBS, NBC, and ABC. TV advertising rose 1000 percent and the networks made millions. CBS made a profit of $8.9 million in 1953. By 1957 that number had risen to $22.2 million. Prime-time programming was filled with practically interchangeable situation comedies, quiz shows, and action programs. When critics protested the dumbing down of television, the industry sang out as one voice: "We are only giving the audience what they want."

The First TV Superstar Rises and Falls

Critics notwithstanding, there was no denying that tens of millions of people tuning in every day. And there was no need to persuade the American public that everyone should watch TV. In the early days, those who had televisions would put them in front of their windows with the screens facing the street. Crowds of up to fifty people would gather to watch the action even though they couldn't hear the sound. Intrigued Americans bought TVs as fast as they could be manufactured. Networks and advertisers struggled to keep up with the demand for programming.

Milton Berle in drag. Berle was a vaudeville comic long before he became famous for his role as master of ceremonies for Texaco Star Theater.

Many give the credit for accelerating the sales of televisions to one man. He was a forty-two-year-old vaudeville slapstick comic named Milton Berle. His humor was often vulgar and manic, and depended heavily on sight gags. (Berle was probably the first man

TV Backlash

Small-town America got a glimpse of what people in the big city were watching in 1953, when the country was wired with coaxial cable. Until then, almost all TV audiences were in big cities like New York, Chicago, Philadelphia, and Los Angeles. There was quite a backlash in the heartland. William Boddy writes in *Fifties Television* that a 1951 article in a trade magazine warned: "Off-color jokes, swish routines, and city humor hits the small towns and suburbs with [an] unpleasant impact, focusing reaction upon certain entertainers—and their sponsors." A 1955 book, *Television Program and Production,* complained:

> What is acceptable to broad-minded night club audiences in Manhattan, Hollywood, or Las Vegas is rarely apt to be fare for admission in homes in any city or town. . . . Jaded and liquored celebrants in a night club will accept as sophisticated humor and wit what is actually nothing but smut. . . . What many entertainers fail to realize is that bistros, night spots, and bright lights are only a minute segment of America. And yet they insist on broadcasting to the entire nation comic material which is definitely not acceptable in the average American home. . . . Our nation consists of 160 million citizens, most of whom live in small towns, go to church on Sunday, attempt to bring up their children decently, and do not regard burlesque shows as the ultimate in theater.

One immediate effect of this backlash was to drive comedians like Milton Berle off the air. His ethnic brand of vaudeville humor did not "play well in Peoria."

in America to appear on TV comically dressed as a woman.) Berle would fall on his face, take a pie in it, or don a wig and a dress. There was never a pause in the action, and Berle had perfected his art as a successful comedian for years.

Berle had spent his entire life in the theater, beginning work at the age of six. He applied for a job as master of ceremonies for *Texaco Star Theater* in 1948. At the time there were only a half-million TV sets in America.

Almost from the start, Berle's Tuesday night show was an event. People who did not have televisions visited those who did. The success of the show alone caused setless people to go out and buy their own TVs. The year after the show started, Berle's face was on both *Time* and *Newsweek* magazines; he was television's first superstar.

Berle's show received a 94.7 rating, meaning that 94.7 percent of all televisions were tuned in to his show. Thanks to "Uncle Miltie," NBC was making $41 million a year by 1952. But Berle's ratings soon began to slip. When he started, almost half the televisions in America were in New York City. The rest were in big cities like Boston, Chicago, Philadelphia, and Los Angeles. In 1953 coaxial cable brought smaller towns and villages into the TV audience. Few rural people understood Berle's racy, big-city comedy. By 1955, Berle was off the air.

A young girl watches an early variety show. Well-known classical musicians were regularly featured on these shows, bringing cultural experiences to audiences who would otherwise never experience them.

Other comedians took Berle's place. George Burns and Gracie Allen made the transition from radio to TV. Sid Caesar had a very popular revue called *Your Show of Shows.* His show gave some extremely talented writers their start, including Woody Allen, Mel Brooks, and Neil Simon.

The Golden Age of TV Drama

One of the promises of early TV was "a theater in your home." [44] By 1953 this promise was realized with an impressive group of weekly showcases such as *Kraft Television Theater, Studio One,* and *The Philco TV Playhouse.* The shows sometimes employed famous actors from stage and screen. But more often, the TV dramas introduced emerging young talents such as Rod Steiger, Paul Newman, Marlon Brando, James Dean, Natalie Wood, Mary Martin, and others.

These were creative and exciting times. Young directors, writers, and actors were hired to produce different plays every week. Their counterparts in film could rely on huge budgets, multiple takes, and intricate editing. But TV directors had to handle large casts who performed live. There was no room for mistakes, the show had to wrap up in thirty minutes, and the actors were mostly inexperienced.

Early television dramas opened the door to young playwrights and writers such as Paddy Chayefsky (screen-writer of *Marty* and later *Network*), Gore Vidal, and Rod Serling. (Serling wrote *Requiem for a Heavyweight* and later produced *The Twilight Zone*.) Dramatist David Shaw wrote in 1954, "For the writer, television is a god-send, for here at last is a medium that will give him a chance." [45]

There were, of course, also hun-dreds of plays based on timeworn for-mulas—boy-meets-girl, good-over-evil, love-conquers-all—that filled broadcasting hours. In 1954, eight network shows staged a total of 343 plays. Ten filmed dramas used another 400 scripts.

Some scripts were slightly contro-versial. But the big issues of the day, such as the racial clashes in the South, were treated gingerly. Paddy Chayefsky claimed, "You can't write the Little Rock thing because they can't sell sets down South . . . ." [46]

Reginald Rose described how he was forced to alter his play *Thunder on Sycamore Street* in 1954. The drama about a black family harassed by white racists "was unpalatable to the networks since many of their stations are situated in Southern states, and it was felt that viewers might be appalled at the sight of a Negro as the beleaguered hero of a television drama." [47]

Sometimes the interference could be petty. Aluminum giant (and adver-tiser) Alcoa insisted that a lynching in *Tragedy in a Temporary Town* could not be set in a trailer park, because mobile homes were made of aluminum. The writer had to substitute wooden shacks for aluminum house trailers.

America Loves Lucy

The most popular shows on fifties television were the sitcoms (short for situation comedies). Many of the early shows, such as *The Jack Benny Show* and *Amos 'n' Andy,* were taken directly from the radio. Later shows included bland suburban comedies such as *Father Knows Best, Make Room for Daddy*, and *Leave It to Beaver*. But one of the classics from this era, still enjoyed today, was the off-the-wall antics of *I Love Lucy*.

Lucille Ball was forty years old in 1951 and in the middle of a hum-drum show business career. In the movies she was seen as a comedian as opposed to an actress. She was called "the Queen of the B-Movies" and had a mixed-race marriage to a Cuban bandleader named Desi Arnaz. Lucy played on radio shows, but like Berle, she was a visual comic. She had an expressive face, and was wacky enough to generate sympathy rather than irritation.

In 1950, CBS asked Lucy to do a weekly sitcom. No one had great hopes for the show; if Lucy was supposed to be a dizzy housewife, network executives wanted to pair her with a straight-arrow husband. But Lucy insisted they cast Arnaz as her husband on the show. The people at CBS, from the president on down, were appalled. So were the advertisers. Arnaz, with a thick, Cuban accent, mangled the English language. Executives said no one would believe Lucy was married to a Cuban bandleader. "What do you mean no one will believe it?" she answered. "We *are* married!" [48]

Lucy continued to fight for Arnaz because she understood something: Since Americans knew Desi was her husband and was really a bandleader, no one would know where the show started and reality ended. After a series of setbacks, the show found a sponsor—Philip Morris cigarettes—and premiered on October 15, 1951.

Vivian Vance, Lucille Ball, William Frawley, and Desi Arnaz, the stars of the well-known comedy show I Love Lucy.

Within weeks, *I Love Lucy* was a hit. As many as two out of three televisions were tuned in to her Monday night show. The show was so popular, in fact, that the huge Marshall Field store in Chicago changed its Monday night sales to Thursday. The store put a sign in the window that said: "We love Lucy too so we're closing on

Lucy, in one of her all-time popular shows, tries out for a commercial but has difficulty pronouncing the product's tongue-twisting name.

Monday nights." [49]

I Love Lucy hit a nerve with the American public. One of the writers for the show pointed out that Lucy held a mirror up to every married couple in America. Not a regular mirror "that reflects the truth, nor a magic mirror that portrays fantasy. But a Coney Island kind of mirror that distorts, exaggerates, and makes

vastly amusing every little incident, foible, and idiosyncrasy of married life." [50]

On April 7, 1952, 10.6 million households were tuning in to *I Love Lucy*. No show in history had reached that many people. By 1954 over 50 million watched the show. Its popularity lifted advertisers and CBS, which showed a profit for the first time in 1953. Thanks to Lucy, television became the largest advertising medium in the world in 1955.

Reality intersected with show business when Lucy became pregnant in 1952. Writers wanted to incorporate the pregnancy into the story line, shocking Philip Morris. Pregnant women had never before been seen in films or television. A pregnant comedian seemed in bad taste. Finally Arnaz convinced the advertisers to go along with the concept. But the word *pregnant* was not to be uttered—instead, Lucy was "an expectant mother."

To protect itself, CBS lined up a priest, a minister, and a rabbi to review all the pregnancy scripts. "It looked like a revival meeting around the place," [51] Lucy said. Over 44 million viewers tuned in to the show on which Lucy was to have her baby, twice as many as watched the inauguration of Dwight D. Eisenhower the

A Recipe for a TV Program

While the golden age of television left America with many memorable programs, there was much that was mediocre. Mrs. A. Scott Bullitt, president of King Broadcasting in Seattle, thought the dynamics of such shows could be reduced to a simple recipe. Her speech, quoted in J. Fred MacDonald's *One Nation Under Television*, was given in 1952 to a group of educators and industry officials. Her recipe for a TV program:

> Take 1 cup of Sponsor's Requirements and sift gently, next add 2 tablespoons of Agency Ideas, carefully chilled, and 1/2 dozen Staff Suggestions, well-beaten. However fresh and flavorful, they will curdle when combined with Agency Ideas, so they must be beaten until stiff. Stir together in a smoke-filled room and sprinkle generously with Salesman's Gimmicks.
>
> Cover mixture with a tight lid so that no Imagination can get in and no Gimmicks can get out, and let stand while costs increase.
>
> Then take 1 jigger of Talent, domestic will do.
>
> Flavor with Production Problems
>
> A pinch of Doubt
>
> And, if you have any, a dash of Hope.
>
> Fold these ingredients carefully so they can get into a small studio—a slightest jolt will sour the results.
>
> Place in the oven with your fingers crossed.
>
> Sometimes it comes out a tasty delicacy, and sometimes, it's just cooked.

next day. And Desi Arnaz Jr. was born right on schedule on January 19, 1953.

Kids' Shows

Television shows for kids appeared almost as soon as TV went on the air. The *Howdy Doody Show* started in 1947, featuring Clarabelle the Clown. Other kiddy favorites included *Ding Dong School*, *The Pinky Lee Show*, and *Kukla, Fran, and Ollie*. In 1955, Bob Keeshan, who had played Clarabelle the Clown, started his own show, *Captain Kangaroo*. Keeshan won awards for his show because he put the needs of the children ahead of the demands of the sponsors.

Saturday morning cartoons such as CBS's *Mighty Mouse Playhouse* were first aired in 1955. That year, ABC premiered the hour-long *Mickey Mouse Club*. This program introduced Walt Disney to American children. The show only ran until 1959, but was by far the most popular children's show. Fan mail poured in from across the country at a rate of seventy-five hundred letters a month.

The cast of the Mickey Mouse Club. *Kids across America tuned in to see their favorite mouseketeers perform skits and sing songs.*

Even children's programming, however, could not escape the moralists of the day. A broad move against TV programming occurred in Chicago in mid-1950 when the National Television Review Board was created. According to J. Fred MacDonald:

> Soon the board publicly condemned shows it felt objectionable, among them *Howdy Doody* ("loud . . . confused . . . senseless . . . clown's role too feminine"), *Juvenile Jury* ("bad taste . . . smart-aleck kids should be spanked instead of applauded"), wrestling ("phony contest, unsportsman-

like tactics . . . glorifies sadism"), and *Leave It to the Girls* ("gowns cut too low . . . ridicules marriage . . . excessive frivolity concerning family, authority and customs"). [52]

By 1952 the board issued its Citizens' Television Code, with a twelve-point guide to "what shall be deemed objectionable."

As the fifties ended, television was firmly under the control of sponsors with little inclination to rock the boat. As the hundreds of millions of advertising dollars rolled in, networks gladly subscribed to the television code. Gone were the exciting days of live television and riveting drama. In their place came the escalating violence of adventure shows coupled with the tinny canned laughter of banal sitcoms. But while millions of American eyes were locked onto TV screens, a revolution was taking place in music, literature, movies, and the arts. And except for Elvis Presley and a few rockers, this revolution was definitely not televised.

Chapter Six

Teenagers participate in a rock 'n' roll dance class in New York. Rock 'n' roll became the defining music of the 1950s.

Rock, Writing, and Beatnik Rebellion

The wide acceptance of television affected the entire range of fifties arts and entertainment. From the falling popularity of movies to the rising popularity of rock 'n' roll, television distracted and attracted people's ever-shortening attention spans. While TV was the centerpiece of fifties family life, another louder and more insistent beat that was central to the lives of millions of teens. Rock music painted a wild rainbow of color in an otherwise drab decade.

The reasons for the rock music's successes were varied but much importance could be assigned to the power of radio. When television came along, millions of adults permanently

79

boomer born in 1946 was only nine years old when Elvis hit number one.

Hail! Hail! Rock 'n' Roll

Rock music might be the soundtrack to the fifties, but in fact, until mid-decade, there was no rock 'n' roll. At least it wasn't called by that name. In the early 1950s, the smoky rhythm and blues (R&B) emanating from African American radio stations would have been called "boogie-woogie" or "race music." Gospel-tinged songs with vocal harmonies and little or no instrumental backing was called "doo-wop."

Whatever they called it, white teens from the suburbs were buying African American R&B records. In 1951, a white record store owner in Cleveland, Ohio, noticed this dramatic new trend. He told a local disc jockey named Alan Freed. Freed, who hosted a late-night classical music show, agreed to play some of the wild new records after his classical show was over.

In the summer of 1951, Freed inaugurated *The Moondog Show* on a fifty thousand-watt clear channel in Cleveland. The signal was so strong that it skipped across the stratosphere to a vast area of the Midwest. Teenagers could tune in from rural

Rock 'n' roll disk jockey Alan Freed hosted The Moondog Show, *which broadcast rock 'n' roll throughout the Midwest.*

switched off their radios. Programmers were forced to find a new audience. And radio was about the only place to hear rock 'n' roll. Huge concert halls or arenas did not exist at the time. Radio also prevailed because the audience was so young—a baby

The group Bill Haley and the Comets became well known for mixing the styles of country western and rhythm and blues.

towns, big cities, and suburbs to hear Freed spinning records, chattering wildly, and beating on a Cleveland phone book with a drumstick. To millions of teens isolated in dull, conformist towns, this might as well have been music from outer space.

Instead of calling the music rhythm and blues, Freed used a term from Wild Bill Moore's 1947 hit, "We're Gonna Rock, We're Gonna Roll." Moondog's Rock and Roll Party became an instant success. Freed stuck to the black roots of rock and

helped make stars of such artists as Fats Domino, Johnny Ace, Johnny Otis, the Drifters, the Platters, and the Moonglows. In the meantime, white-owned radio stations tried to distract teens with wimpy rock ballads such as Kay Starr's "Rock and Roll Waltz."

In 1953 a white ex-country singer named Bill Haley crossed rhythm and blues with country music and pioneered a new sound. When Bill Haley and the Comets released "Crazy Man Crazy," the song's blend of R&B and country became one of the first rock

Rebellion on the Silver Screen

Rock 'n' roll fired a rebellious attitude in white teenagers who chafed under conformity. Adding fuel to this fire were several crucial films that capitalized on a growing trend called juvenile delinquency. The first such film, *The Wild One*, starred Marlon Brando. Released in 1954, the movie is about the leader of a motorcycle gang that rampages through a town. Brando's character, dressed in a black leather jacket and blue jeans, hides his sensitive nature behind a macho façade. In one of the film's most famous exchanges, a local girl asks Brando, "What are you rebelling against?" and Brando replies, "Waddaya got?" Millions of teens instantly identified with Brando's tough-guy character with a heart of gold. Young men began to imitate Brando's dress and manner.

The next year, James Dean starred in *Rebel Without a Cause*, about a middle-class teen in a hostile school environment who lives with uncaring parents. In this movie, Dean's character muses, "If I could have just one day when I wasn't all confused . . . I wasn't ashamed of everything. If I felt I belonged someplace." *Rebel Without a Cause* became a favorite movie for alienated teens who blamed the world's injustices on their parents'

Marlon Brando stars in The Wild One. *Brando and James Dean became teen idols by playing bad boys with sensitive streaks.*

generation. Dean died on September 30, 1955, in the wreck of his Porsche in California. His death at the height of his career made him a cult hero to teens the world over.

hits. Haley had another hit the next year with "Shake, Rattle, and Roll."

In the spring of 1955, MGM released the movie *The Blackboard Jungle*, about a high school teacher confronted by rebellious, violent students. The opening credits rolled to

Bill Haley and the Comets' "Rock Around the Clock." It created a nationwide sensation. Overexcited teens rioted in some theaters. The movie was called "degenerate," but Haley's song shot to number one and the rock era had begun. By the summer of 1955, the record had sold a million copies.

The Texas-born Haley didn't invent rock 'n' roll, but he took the African-inspired beat of rhythm and blues, stripped away the sexual lyrics, harmonious backing, and blues inflection in the singing. Then he added a guitar track and other effects from what was known as "hillbilly" music. Though his career didn't last long, Haley was one of the first white rock superstars.

Elvis Presley Rocks

By 1955 black artists were enjoying unprecedented success. Chuck Berry's "Maybellene" was a number-one hit, closely followed by Little Richard's "Tutti Frutti." Black music was so popular, in fact, that record producer Sam Phillips said, "If I could find a white man with a Negro sound, I could make billions of dollars." [53] Very soon, Phillips found his man—Elvis Presley.

Elvis Presley looked both tough and sensual, with greased-back hair and a leather jacket. Beneath it all he was a religious country boy from Tupelo, Mississippi. He was also white, and "safe" for the adoration of millions of teenage girls called "bobby soxers."

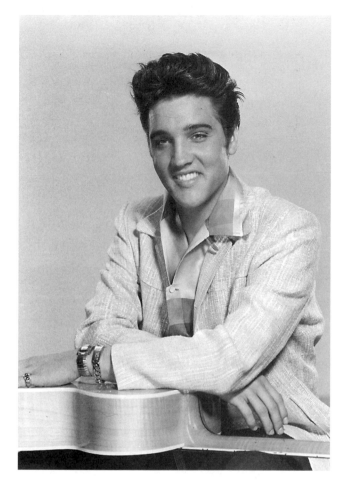

Elvis Presley became famous for his flamboyant singing style and personality.

Elvis came along when the pop music in America was dominated by syrupy orchestral arrangements and crooning singers dressed in sweaters or formal clothes. Presley's emotion-charged "Heartbreak Hotel" shot to the top of *Billboard* magazine's charts on April 21, 1956. Sharing the top five that week were the squeaky clean Perry Como and an instrumental by the Nelson Riddle Orchestra. Other hits that April included "Love Is a Many Splendored Thing" and "The Yellow Rose of Texas," by Mitch Miller.

Elvis followed "Heartbreak Hotel" with a string of hits that made him a household name. For fifty-five of the next one hundred weeks, Elvis would have the best-selling records in America with "Hound Dog," "Don't Be Cruel," "All Shook Up," "Love Me Tender," and others. But middle America was still not ready for Elvis. When he appeared on Ed Sullivan's TV variety show, he was shown only from the waist up. His bump-and-grind dancing was deemed too sensual for mass consumption.

Elvis took to wearing gold lamé suits and driving around in gold Cadillac convertibles. But he maintained his humble roots, at least in public. When asked if his music might be contributing to juvenile delinquency, he said: "If I thought that was true, I would quit and go back to driving a truck. I wouldn't do anything to hurt anybody." When asked about his hold over young people he replied, "You tell me, I don't know. I was asked that question before and I've been thinking about it ever since." [54]

Elvis influenced hundreds of thousands of kids to pick up guitars and learn to sing and play. Guitar sales in 1950 were about 228,000. By 1959 that number had jumped to 400,000.

Rock 'n' Roll Backlash

As the popularity of rock 'n' roll grew, so did opposition to the music. The so-called objectionable content of rock songs triggered fierce parental and religious campaigns against the songs. A series of songs by a group called the Midnighters was used to lead the charge. The barely hidden euphemisms for sex in songs like "Work With Me Annie," "Sexy Ways," and "Annie Had a Baby," were used to condemn all rock music.

Rock music was banned from many radio stations. In some towns rock records were broken, piled up, and burned. "Smash the records you possess which present a pagan culture and pagan concept of life," urged the newspaper of the Catholic Youth Center. "Some songwriters need a good swift kick. So do some singers. So do some disc jockeys." These incitements to violence had an effect. DJs were fired for playing black artists' records. Law enforcement agencies banned rock and R&B concerts, especially those where blacks performed with whites on the same stage. In the

South, White Citizens' Councils spoke out against "bop and savage Negro music." When Elvis performed at the Pan Pacific auditorium in Los Angeles, he was ordered to "clean up his show or else." [55]

Of course, when the police pushed, teenagers pushed back. At a rock show in Boston, police upset the crowd by turning on the house lights and interrupting the concert. Afterwards, members of the audience went on a spree, breaking windows and brawling. One boy was killed, others severely beaten. The show's producer, Alan Freed, was charged with inciting a riot and anarchy; it took him several years and a great deal of money to get the trumped-up charges thrown out of court.

Before long the red-baiters in Congress found a new target. Congress decided to investigate the music industry and found that record companies paid disc jockeys bribes to play certain records. This practice—dubbed payola—was common throughout the music industry at the time, but Congress chose to investigate only rock 'n' roll music. Alan Freed became the target of a payola investigation. Congressional investigators assumed that rock was "evil, ugly, unintelligible, and bad, and that teen-

Not everyone endorsed the new rock 'n' roll music. Many of the older generation found it offensive and even dangerous for teens. Here, a woman protests outside the RCA building.

agers were passive victims who never would have listened to it unless it had been forced upon them by illegal activity." [56]

The payola scandal ruined Freed. He was blacklisted from radio and drank himself to death in 1965 at the age of forty-three. After the payola hearings, rock music lost another voice when Elvis was drafted into the army in 1959. That year Little Richard found religion and quit rocking to preach the gospel.

A series of other events tarnished rock's image. Chuck Berry was arrested for transporting a fourteen-year-old girl across state lines (Berry claimed he was set up by police). Rocker Jerry Lee Lewis married his thirteen-year-old cousin, outraging most Americans and ruining his career.

Perhaps the single event that most dramatically marked the end of the 1950s rock era was the night in February 1959 that an airplane carrying Buddy Holly, Richie Valens, and the Big Bopper crashed into an Iowa cornfield, killing all three. By 1960, seminal rock 'n' roll had faded away. The new stars were clean-cut, white teenage crooners such as Fabian, Frankie Avalon, and Paul Anka.

As the fifties ended, rock 'n' roll had not brought about the much-feared widespread youth rebellion, but it had united teens and set them apart as a group from their parents. Once a teenager broke off from the music of adults, questioning of other values was inevitable. The quiet hum of a conformist and complacent suburban world was shattered by the insistent beat of rock 'n' roll.

The Beat Generation

Although rock music got most of the attention, there were other types of popular music in the fifties. The clean-cut Kingston Trio performed folk ballads accompanied by acoustic guitars and banjo. One of the greatest folk groups of the era was the Weavers, led by Pete Seeger. Their highballing four-part harmonies were seen by some as a welcome alternative to Elvis.

The careers of many of the greatest legends in jazz peaked in the fifties. Miles Davis, Charlie Parker, Lester Young, Dizzy Gillespie, Dave Brubeck, and others could be found performing in jazz clubs in America's big cities, and jazz records sold in respectable numbers.

Jazz was popular among African Americans, but it was also the music of the so-called Beat generation centered in New York City, San Francisco, and other large cities. ("Beat" originally meant cheated or emotionally drained, but was reinvented to mean beatific or at peace. The term was later expanded to "beatnik." Before the term came along, artistic nonconformists were called bohemians.)

Beats were among the first to protest the blandness and conformity of the era. While most Americans moved to the suburbs, the Beats were urban pioneers of what would later become the counterculture. They saw suburbia as a prison and saw themselves as poets in a land of materialism.

The original Beats came together in New York City. They were students at Columbia University in the 1940s who were shunned by conventionally popular and successful students. Allen Ginsberg was an awkward, shy, seventeen-year-old homosexual from New Jersey when he met Lucien Carr, a well-to-do kid from St. Louis. Carr introduced Ginsberg to William Burroughs, whose prominent grandfather had invented the adding machine. Burroughs graduated from Harvard in 1936, but propelled by his deep alienation, his drug use, and his homosexuality, he lived a subterranean life in Greenwich Village. Into this mix of poets and thinkers came Jack Kerouac, who had come to Columbia on a football scholarship but became a novelist when he injured his knee. Later they were joined by a hyperactive madman from Denver named Neal Cassady.

The Beats came together over bottles of cheap wine and books of verse by French poets such as Flaubert, Baudelaire, and Rimbaud. They spoke

American poet Allen Ginsberg was part of the Beat movement. Beats invented their own subculture, which was centered in Greenwich Village, New York.

of a "new vision"—a society of artist-citizens in which they would be leaders. They recorded their thoughts and dreams on reams of paper.

According to writer John Cellon Holmes in his book *Go*, the Beats

Catcher in the Rye

One of the most popular rebels of fifties literary fiction was Holden Caulfield. Caulfield, a teenager who skips out of prep school to loiter in New York, is the troubled hero of J. D. Salinger's *Catcher in the Rye.* Published in 1951, the book spoke directly to adolescents who felt they were sensitive, spiritual souls trapped in a vulgar world. According to Douglas T. Miller and Marion Nowak, in *The Fifties: The Way We Really Were:*

> Holden Caulfield, in *Catcher,* is literally nauseated by the physicality of his universe. Sounds, smells, appearances assault and sicken him. The characters exist in a banal America controlled by the insensitive and crude. The drunks, boors, and phonies of Holden Caulfield's world are all simplistic but typical characters. Salinger made it very easy for the reader to concur in sneering at this vulgar, repressive society. Simultaneously he flatters his audience; he pretends both reader and protagonist share an intelligence, sensitivity, and savvy far superior to that of the common folk.

Salinger's thin book graced the bookshelves of countless college dormitories and continues to sell by the millions to this day.

lived in a world of

> dingy backstairs pads—Times Square cafeterias, bebop joints, nightlong wanderings, meetings on street corners, hitchhiking, a myriad of "hip" bars all over the city, and the streets themselves. It was inhabited by people "hung up" with drugs and other habits, searching out a new degree of craziness. They were going all the time, living at night, rushing around to "make contact," suddenly disappearing into jail or on the road, only to turn up again and search one another out. They had a view that life was underground, mysterious, and they seemed unaware of anything outside the reality of deals, a pad to stay in, "digging the frantic jazz," and keeping everything going. [57]

Beats were fascinated with black urban culture. They used words like *hip, dig, cool, man,* and *split.* They saw themselves as white bopsters and believed blacks were somehow freer and less burdened by "straight" America.

Drugs were important to the Beats, viewed as a key to the spiritual world. They took a widely available amphetamine called benzedrine or "bennies," which kept them awake (and writing or driving) for days. They also smoked marijuana, known as "tea" in those days. Some, like Burroughs, fell into heroin addiction.

Jack Kerouac and Allen Ginsberg

Of all the Beat writers, Jack Kerouac was the most prolific. He wrote his books on huge rolls of white butcher paper, which he could feed nonstop into his typewriter. Kerouac could also be seen wandering around the city recording his observations of life around him. He called it "sketching." When others read Kerouac's words, they were amazed by his natural instinct for unstructured, flowing prose. In *The Lonesome Traveler*, Kerouac gives his vision of patrons in a New York City bar:

> Men do love bars and good bars should be loved.—It's full of businessmen, workmen, Finn MacCools of Time.—Be-overalled oldgray topers dirty and beerswiggin glad.—Nameless truck busdrivers with flashlights slung from their hips.—Old beatfaced beerswallowers sadly upraising purple lips to happy drinking ceilings.—This is great New York Third Avenue, free lunch, smells of Moody street exhaust river lunch in road of grime bysmashing the

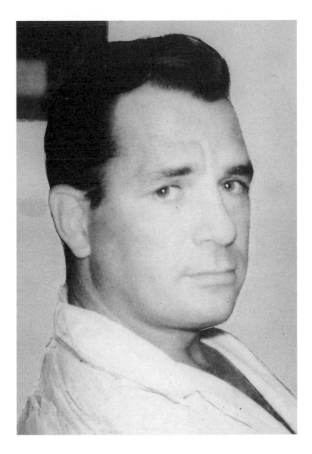

Jack Kerouac was the most prolific of the Beat writers. He is best known for his book On the Road, *about his travels across America.*

door, guitarplaying long sideburned heroes smell out there on wood doorsteps in afternoon drowse. [58]

After Kerouac's first book, *The Town and the City*, was published in 1950, the author spent six years "writing whatever came into my head, hopping freights, hitch-hiking, and working as a railroad brakeman, deckhand and scullion on merchant ships, government fire lookouts, and hundreds of assorted jobs." [59] *On the Road* , published in 1957 (five years after it was written), brought Kerouac immediate fame and acclaim. He was credited with being the voice of the Beat generation. Other books came in quick succession and were translated into eighteen languages.

Before long, the original Beats abandoned New York for what they perceived as even more free-spirited San Francisco. The literary headquarters for the Beats was the City Lights bookstore, owned by poet and publisher Lawrence Ferlinghetti. In 1955, Ferlinghetti agreed to publish Ginsberg's first work, *Howl*, a lengthy poem described as poetry "done to the rhythms and phrases of modern jazz—a tragic custard-pie comedy of wild phrasing, meaningless images for the beauty of abstract poetry of mind." [60]

On October 13, 1955, Ginsberg gave a historic reading of *Howl*. The first line is one of the most famous in American poetry: "I saw the best minds of my generation / destroyed by madness / starving, mystical, naked, / who dragged themselves thru the angry streets at / dawn look-

ing for a negro fix." [61] Ginsberg gave a dazzling performance that night. It was a triumph for the author and for Beat writers in general. Within a few years, Beat writers would become best-selling authors and Beat visions of an alternative lifestyle would be extremely popular among teenagers and college students.

Beatnik Backlash

Powerful conservative elements were not about to let a group of bearded beatniks corrupt America's youth. Beat poetry, like rock 'n' roll, was dismissed as supporting "promiscuous individual freedom at the expense of social regularity." Jack Kerouac's writing was labeled as "vulgar ramblings on a latrine wall." Another critic wrote, "We are witnessing a revolt of all the forces hostile to civilization itself." The Beats "compromise a movement of brute stupidity and know-nothingism that is trying to take over the country." [62]

A 1959 *Life* issue included a typical media attack on the Beats in an article titled "The Only Rebellion Around":

The wide public belief that the Beats are simply dirty people in sandals is only a small but repellent part of the truth. Their philosophy was created solely to offend the whole population. The three classes of people who become Beats are sick little bums; the amateur or weekend Beats; and hostile little females. [63] The article went on to complain that Beats were either black or befriended blacks. Some were political radicals. All were sexually promiscuous, and 60 percent were emotionally unstable. The article departed from the magazine's famous factual photorealism and created a photo spread in a studio illustrating "uncomfortable living Beat-style." "Photos showed a black-clad Beat 'chick,' a Charlie Parker record, Chianti (wine) bottles, a bare mattress, orange crates, bongos, and beer cans for the pitiful baby to play with. As *Life* put it the photos were 'recreated in the studio using paid models.'" [64]

Authorities were prepared to do more than shake their heads in disapproval. In 1957 two San Francisco police officers walked into City Lights and bought copies of *Howl* and three other publications they deemed obscene. They arrested Ferlinghetti. The *Howl* trial fascinated America. The

Beatniks enjoy themselves at the Cock and Bull in Greenwich Village. The Beats broke with many of the conventions of the 1950s, experimenting with sex and drugs.

American Civil Liberties Union (ACLU) defended Ginsberg's work, submitting to the court positive reviews in the *New York Times*, and called on well-known figures in the world of letters to testify to the poem's importance, power, and legitimacy. In 1957 *Howl* was ruled not obscene. In fact, the judge wrote:

The first part of *Howl* presents a picture of a nightmare world; the

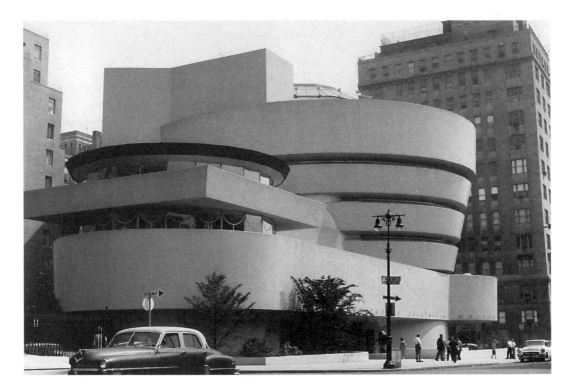

The Guggenheim Museum in 1959, the year of its opening. Designed by Frank Lloyd Wright, the building's design was considered radically unconventional.

second part is an indictment of those elements of modern society destructive of the best qualities of human nature; such elements are predominantly identified as materialism, conformity, and the mechanization leading to war. . . . It ends with a plea for holy living. [65]

After the obscenity trial, the publishing contracts began to roll in for the Beats. Kerouac found fame to be destructive and ended his life in a cloud of alcohol in 1969. But Ginsberg became an American man of letters. The City Lights bookstore became a mecca to Beats from across the world. It was a sure sign that the walls of the old order were cracking.

Creating a New Vision and Language

While Beat poets and rock 'n' roll music were making a lot of noise, a quieter revolution was taking place in the studios and museums of New York City. World War II had shifted the capital of bohemian life and the avant-garde from Paris to New York. Many famous abstract-expressionist artists moved to America after the war, including Marc Chagall, Max Ernst, and Piet Mondrian. Along with Jackson Pollock, Willem de Kooning and others, they became known as the New York School of painting.

One of the principal patrons of the New York School was heiress Peggy Guggenheim. In 1959 the Guggenheim Museum opened in New York City; designed by Frank Lloyd Wright, the building was a multilevel spiral, and museumgoers followed the art along an incline from the ground floor to the top. The structure remains one of the most remarkable art museums, and works of architecture, in the world.

People continue to view the fifties as a bland, homogenized decade, but the wild colors of the expressionist painters blended with the visionary words of the Beat poets over the soundtrack of jazz and rock music. Whoever chose to turn off the TV and head out into the "neon night" could find a world that turned *Leave It to Beaver* America upside down.

Painter Jackson Pollock

Twentieth-century giants Pablo Picasso and Henri Matisse were still alive in the fifties. But the most-talked-about innovator of modern painting was an American back-woodsman from Wyoming named Jackson Pollock. As Peter Lewis writes in his book *The Fifties,* "Despite Pollock's wild reputation, he was no primitive. He had deliberately suppressed his artistic training to create a new visual language. His own description of his methods could hardly be more explicit":

> My painting is not done on the easel. I prefer to put it up on a wall or better still spread it out on the floor. When the canvas is on the floor, I feel as if I am part of the painting. I can walk around it and work from all sides, literally be in the painting. . . . I have eliminated the usual tools of the painter. I prefer sticks, a trowel, ordinary spoons or just to let the liquid color drip or spatter . . . . When I am painting, I have no knowledge of what I'm doing. Only after a moment of returning to consciousness do I become aware of what I have been about.

Pollock, whom the press dubbed "Jack the Dripper," was also an alcoholic who perished in a car accident in 1956.

Chapter Seven

Automobile design in the fifties utilized flashy chrome and wraparound windshields inspired by fighter jets.

Technology and Science

The nuclear age began with an atomic inferno over Japan. But wartime technology meant to destroy also helped usher in the most creative scientific era the world had ever known. The fifties were a time of many technological firsts. Scientists sythesized wonder drugs that ended a plague of diseases. They invented huge computers to unravel age-old mathematical problems in minutes. They created transistors that changed electronics—and the way we live— forever.

Using missile technology developed for war, scientists launched communications satellites. With technology developed to build fighter jets, they built sleeker, faster cars and began cross-country passenger jet service. Even radioactive nuclear isotopes were put to peaceful uses in medicine and energy production.

Oak Ridge Laboratory in Tennessee, where scientists manufactured the first atomic weapons.

Of course, this technology came at a price. Bigger cars plugged highways and polluted the air. Nuclear testing spread radioactivity across the land. New pesticides destroyed beneficial insects, birds, fish, and even people along with pests. And the garbage from America's brand-new throwaway society piled up in junkyards and dumps from coast to coast.

To the average person in the fifties, however, it was a miraculous age of discovery. The new technology touched everyone. Children watching television were able to clock the countdowns of U.S. space flights. Common people discussed the nuclear physics of fission and fusion. And the world rejoiced when modern medicine wiped out smallpox, yellow fever, and polio. Scientists, whose image had been absentminded tinkerers, became the new heroes in postwar America.

The Nuclear Age

The era of scientific discovery has been called the nuclear age. As soon as the first atomic bomb was exploded, scientists began harnessing the immense power of the atom for peaceful purposes. U.S. scientists convinced politicians that civilians, not the military, should be in charge of atomic programs. Consequently, a five-member association named the Atomic Energy Commission (AEC) was formed in the late 1940s. Its mission was to plan and construct atomic power plants and to design and build

Nuclear power gained prominence in the 1950s for both its wartime and peacetime uses. Nuclear energy was used to power the first nuclear submarine, the Nautilus.

Nuclear power plants were the primary civilian outgrowth of weapons production. The development of the first nuclear bomb required scientists to build a nuclear reactor to produce weapons-grade material. After the war, reactors were built in Oak Ridge, Tennessee, and Hanford, Washington, to produce plutonium for bombs. The technology required to design, build, and operate these plants was developed in a very short time—less than three years—and provided the knowledge that was the driving force behind the development of commercial nuclear energy.

At first this knowledge was used to develop nuclear-powered submarines capable of extended naval voyages without refueling. The first nuclear submarine, the *Nautilus*, was launched in 1954. An outstanding success, the ship's reactor was the prototype for the first commercial nuclear power plant, built in Shippingport, Pennsylvania, in 1957.

Other nations joined in a search for peaceful uses of atomic energy. Britain had entered into the production of nuclear-fueled electricity in 1956. The first Soviet nuclear power

atomic weapons, described as the biggest single construction job in history. In 1953, Eisenhower ordered nuclear information declassified in his "Atoms for Peace" speech at the United Nations, allowing for wider research into nuclear power.

Nuclear power plants were seen as a miraculous way to harness the power of the atom and make electricity "too cheap to be metered." Burning one pound of coal in a power plant produced one kilowatt-hour of power. One pound of uranium produced 3 million kilowatt-hours (along with radioactive by-products).

Nuclear Factory Dangers

While the media played up the positive side of nuclear power, plants producing weapons-grade plutonium repeatedly released poison into America's environment. According to a December 19, 1989, article in the *Washington Post* by R. Jeffrey Smith:

> A factory producing plutonium for nuclear weapons repeatedly emitted airborne particles of the cancer-causing substance in the vicinity of Hanford, Wash., during the late 1940s and early 1950s, but decided not to warn workers and nearby residents because "nothing was to be gained."
>
> The documents indicate that billions of radioactive particles were emitted each month by the Hanford plant, but that the government was slow to correct the problem. The documents are the latest in a series of revelations about poor safety practices at the 17 facilities involved in the production of nuclear weapons, which experts say have led to widespread environmental problems that will cost hundreds of billions of dollars to clean up.
>
> Sen. John Glenn (D-Ohio) said it shows that "the U.S. nuclear weapons program was exposing large numbers of workers to potentially dangerous health risks but did nothing to warn them and swept the problem under the carpet."
>
> Some of the largest emissions between 1952 and 1954 reached Spokane, 115 miles northeast of Hanford, the documents indicated. The emissions, which included other radioactive substances besides plutonium, were in addition to the deliberate release of radioactive iodine and xenon into the air at Hanford in 1949 as part of an experiment conducted for unknown reasons by the U.S. Air Force.

plant came on-line in 1954, and the French began construction of their first commercial plants in 1957. By the early 1960s nuclear power had been established as a viable commercial energy source.

The Other Side of the Nuclear Coin

Nuclear power plants produce large amounts of radioactive waste, which remains hazardous to humans for up to ten thousand years. When the AEC embarked on a crash course of nuclear plant construction, many safety concerns were brushed aside. The wastes generated at Hanford and Oak Ridge were stored in open pits and basins, shallow burial pits, or large metal tanks that leaked (and still leak). The result was highly contaminated soil and groundwater.

Buying Shoes with Radioactive Tools

By the early fifties, people were willing to use nuclear materials for just about anything. One sign of that was the Shoe-Fitting Fluoroscopes that were installed in all the most modern shoe stores. Kids who were getting new shoes stepped up on a boxlike machine, inserted their feet into an opening at the base, and saw the bones of their feet lit up within the outlines of their new shoes. As they wriggled their toes, salesmen and parents took turns looking through a viewer to determine—scientifically—if the shoes fit properly.

The machine was called a Foot-O-Scope and used X rays to examine the feet of children. Marketed by the United Shoe Machinery Corp., it was used "because young children are not usually able to give the shoe man accurate advice as to how the shoe feels on the foot."

According to Susan Jonas and Marilyn Nissenson in *Going, Going, Gone*:

Typically, a thin plate of aluminum was interposed between the X-ray tube and the foot to lessen X-ray dosage. In most stores, the fluoroscope was operated by a person with no knowledge of X-ray hazards. Some emitted fifty times the radiation rate of a modern hospital fluoroscope. Moreover there was no way of monitoring customers who went from store to store trying on shoes.

Eventually the machines were banned for safety reasons. Salespeople then had to rely on the unscientific thumb-and-forefinger method to determine if the shoe fit.

In spite of the problems, fifties thinkers saw hundreds of uses for nuclear power. Today, some of those ideas seem almost quaint. David Sarnoff, head of RCA, predicted small atomic generators for every home. "Before 1980, ships, aircraft, locomotives, and even automobiles will be atomically fueled," [66] predicted Willard Libby, head of the AEC. Libby envisioned the use of small nuclear bombs to move earth to gouge out harbors and canals, and strip-mine mountains for minerals. *Holiday* magazine wrote: "Perhaps not tomorrow, but maybe the day after, there will be a fission-powered society of less work, more leisure." [67] Left unaddressed was the fact that uranium and plutonium are some of the most poisonous elements on earth.

Medical Wonders

Not only could radioactive elements be used to produce power, they could be used to heal the sick, as well. For the first time, in the fifties radioactive isotopes were used to diagnose disease and to treat cancer.

Perhaps no area of research enjoyed such a broad range of discovery during the fifties than medical science. The discovery of penicillin in 1941 saved untold lives during World War II. By the mid-1950s medical researchers had studied some thirty-five hundred other antibiotics and had introduced seventeen for use in treating human illness. These antibiotics cured everything from rheumatic fever to pneumonia to tuberculosis. Researchers also developed vaccines against a host of childhood illnesses such as measles.

Wiping Out Polio

Perhaps the greatest medical conquest was that over polio. Paralytic poliomyelitis was one of the most frightening of epidemics. After the war, the number of cases grew steadily, and its victims were usually children. Americans all knew about the disease because it had affected one of the most popular presidents, Franklin Delano Roosevelt. Polio was a medical oddity that baffled researchers for years. The infectious agent was spread through contact with a polio patient or by contact with mucus or human feces. Young children were the most susceptible and the most effective

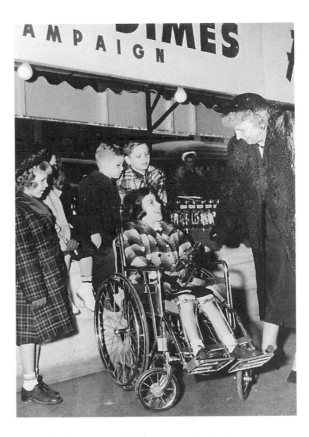

One of the many children permanently damaged by the ravages of polio. Polio epidemics were mysterious and terrifying, afflicting thousands of children and adults.

spreaders of the disease, but older persons could also be stricken. Polio caused paralysis and, often, permanent deformity and disability.

The first polio epidemic was in 1916, when over twenty-seven thousand cases of the disease occurred in twenty states. New York was hardest hit, with nine thousand cases that

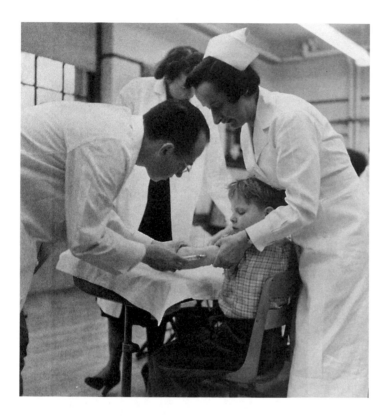

Dr. Jonas Salk injects a boy with his new polio vaccine. The polio vaccine program was the most extensive in history.

the recurrence of this frightful visitor. By 1952 polio was killing more children than any other communicable disease. To combat this menace, the March of Dimes was formed to raise funds for research. The organization contributed over $67 million a year toward a cure; over 100 million Americans made annual donations to the March of Dimes.

This was the situation when a young medical doctor, Jonas Salk, developed a polio vaccine in 1954. In elaborate human trials, Salk's vaccine was given to more than 1 million schoolchildren; another million were given a placebo (a harmless subsitute), and a third million were simply tracked but given no medicine.

The mass polio vaccination was the most extensive program in history, involving more than over 20,000 physicians, 64,000 school personnel, and 220,000 volunteers. The volunteers came from the PTA, the American Legion, the National Council of Catholic Women, and elsewhere. It was the largest peacetime mobilization of its kind. Gallup polls showed that more Americans knew

resulted in twenty-four hundred deaths and a high rate of permanent paralysis. The public reaction was panic; many people fled the cities, which actually helped spread the disease. Winter weather froze the virus and brought a temporary end to the plague.

For the next forty years, urban citizens were terrified every summer by

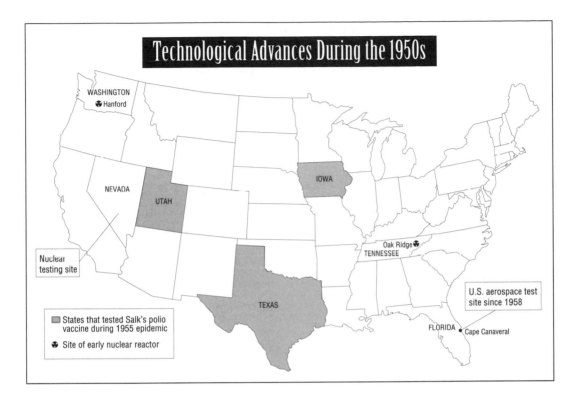

Technological Advances During the 1950s

about the test than could give the full name of president Dwight David Eisenhower.

The effort was closely monitored. On April 12, 1955, the vaccine was declared safe and effective. It was a victory for the entire country. "People observed moments of silence, rang bells, honked horns, blew factory whistles, fired salutes, kept their red lights red in brief periods of tribute, took the rest of the day off, closed their schools, or convoked fervid assemblies therein, drank toasts, hugged children, attended church, smiled at strangers, forgave enemies." [68]

Salk became famous overnight. He was offered a ticker tape parade in New York City but turned it down. He received a presidential citation, the nation's first Congressional Medal for Distinguished Civilian Service, and honorary degrees by the score.

By 1962 polio had virtually disappeared. Only 910 cases were reported in the United States that year, down from 37,476 in 1954. Salk was rewarded with his own research institute in La Jolla, California. Polio was conquered, and it was a victory that the whole nation had helped to bring about, either by volunteering for the

Fifties Computers

Another peaceful spin-off of the nuclear weapons program was the development of computers. Builders of the H-bomb desperately needed a machine that would help them develop trajectory tables and other essential data for new weapons systems. In the forties, researchers at the University of Pennsylvania built the Electronic Numerical Integrator and Calculator (ENIAC). ENIAC used 18,000 standard vacuum tubes, occupied 15,000 square feet of floor space, and consumed about 180,000 watts of electrical power. It could complete five thousand calculations per second. ENIAC was considered a miracle worker military scientists in the early fifties.

By the mid-1950s, ENIAC had turned into UNIVAC, the Universal Automatic Computer. UNIVAC became the first commercially available stored-program electronic digital computer. As the years passed, UNIVAC became faster, more reliable, and easier to operate as transistors replaced tubes. These machines were very expensive to purchase or to rent and were extremely expensive to operate. They were usually found in large computer centers operated by industry and government.

A woman poses with one of the most fantastic inventions of the 1950s, the UNIVAC computer. Although the machine was huge, it performed far fewer functions than today's personal computers.

vaccination program or contributing to the March of Dimes.

V-8s and Tailfins

There was no more obvious a symbol of the fifties than the automobile. Not only was the automobile changing lives, but it was changing the American landscape, as well. One of the most important pieces of legislation of the 1950s would forever alter the look and the feel of the United States. This was the federal Interstate Highway Act of 1956, a bill providing for the construction of forty-one thousand miles of freeways, to be built over a ten-year period, at a cost of $26 billion. The act was one of the largest public construction projects ever undertaken in the United States. Ultimately, it lasted more than twenty-five years and cost over $100 billion.

The highways were necessary because of the record number of cars on the road. From 1950 onward, more than 8 million cars were sold every year. By 1958, almost 68 million cars and trucks were in use—more than one for every household in the United States. Total vehicle miles traveled jumped from 458 billion in 1950 to 800 billion in 1960. And the cars people drove guzzled more gas and spewed more pollution as they got longer and heavier each year.

Automobile design of the 1940s was rounded and humped. In the 1950s, inspired by designs of airplanes and jets of the world war, automakers turned out flashy cars with wraparound windshields, vast expanses of chrome, V-8 engines, and pointy tailfins crowned with giant red taillights. The interiors were filled with new options like radios, air conditioners, padded dashboards, and elegant upholstery. The American public was mesmerized.

The partially completed Hollywood–Santa Ana freeway, one of the first superhighways ever built. Freeways were built in response to America's growing car culture.

American carmakers focused on style, not safety. In 1956 the director of style at General Motors told *Fortune* magazine "Safe cars appeal only to squares, and there ain't any squares no more." [69] Highway deaths mounted—over forty thousand a year by the late fifties. Seat belts were an

Buicks, Oldsmobiles, and Pontiacs roll off the assembly line in 1955. As the number of cars mounted, so did the number of accidents, as automobile manufacturers had little concern for improving cars' safety features.

Crusaders for safety improvements met stiff resistance from the automobile industry; the "big three" automakers were the biggest fish in the corporate sea, and spawned thousands of other businesses. Steel, rubber, gasoline, and construction industries were all dependent on cars. Factor in motels, garages, drive-ins, and tourism and it is easy to see how the automobile culture fueled the American economy.

And oil fueled the cars. During the war, vast new pipelines and large refineries were built to reach and process America's vast domestic oil reserves. Oil consumption nearly doubled during the fifties. The era was marked by gas wars among filling stations, fighting for customers by putting their prices a half-cent per gallon lower than their neighboring stations.

Plastics and Pesticides

The glut of oil fueled a huge chemical industry whose motto was "Better Living through Chemistry." Not only did oil feed cars and industry, but chemical magicians were creating a whole new world using plastics. As with many other advancements, research into plastic compounds accelerated during the war. After the

option available at extra cost but rarely purchased. Standard tires, brakes, and suspension became inadequate as cars got bigger, longer, and lower to the ground. Sharpened, pointy bumpers and tailfins were lethal weapons when accidents occurred.

Life Under the Black Smoke

Steel was the lifeblood of fifties America, an essential component of railroads, cars, and airplanes. Steel supported modern skyscrapers and river-spanning bridges. Most of the steel came from cities around the Great Lakes such as Cleveland, Buffalo, Pittsburgh, and Gary, Indiana. In Pittsburgh alone, more than a dozen steel mills pumped out a steady stream of black coal smoke, visible ash, and residue. The air was so polluted that one British visitor called it "hell with the lid off." As Susan Jonas and Marilyn Nissenson write in *Going, Going, Gone*:

> The sky was always orange. Streetlights came on at noon. One man recalled, "we'd leave for school in the morning with clean clothes and get there covered with soot." When a blast furnace "slipped," tons of grime would be blown out the top of the furnace, and a dark blizzard would descend. Laundry drying on the line, fresh paint on the front porch, even the newspaper spread open on the desk turned black in an instant.

In 1948, a terrible five-day smog darkened the skies of Donora, a small town up the valley [from Pittsburgh]. Families huddled in their homes, afraid to go outside where they could not catch their breath. Half the town's population was stricken with respiratory disease, and five people died before the winds changed and cleared the air.

Added to this smoke was pollution from countless refineries and chemical plants. A number of laws, including the Clean Air Acts of 1963, 1970, and 1990, have vastly improved air quality since the fifties. Pittsburgh, by the way, has been voted America's most livable city several times since 1985.

war, these compounds, which were lightweight, malleable, and easy to produce started showing up in all aspects of modern life. From brightly colored kitchen chairs to telephones to Elvis records, it was hard to remember a world where there was no plastic.

Plastic wasn't the only new chemcial making its way into American life. After World War II the American chemical industry received German research data that revealed the basic chemistry and pesticidal properties of the organophosphate compounds, many of which were developed as chemical weapons during World Wars I and II. The chemical industry immediately developed dozens of compounds that could be used as pesticides and herbicides. Application of these compounds on farm crops increased tenfold.

Pesticides and fertilizers, along with modernized farm equipment, allowed people in the fifties to

A farmer poses with the mound of farm chemicals he uses in an average year. Though the new chemicals boosted farm production, their effect on the environment was largely unknown.

all, an organic pesticide called DDT, was as prevalent in the fifties as automobile tailfins. In 1940 a Swiss scientist named Paul Müller was looking for a way to control household moths. He unearthed some research done in 1870 for a chlorinated hydrocarbon called DDT (dichloro-diphenyl-trichloroethane). The scientist found that when DDT was sprayed on a surface, any bug that landed there for the next six months died. The chemical attacked the insect's nervous system but had little observable effect on warm-blooded mammals (like humans). And it was cheap to manufacture.

DDT was put to immediate use to kill lice on soldiers, civilians, and prisoners of war during World War II. People were overjoyed to be rid of the plague of bugs that had historically been one of their worst torments. The chemical also proved effective in slaughtering mosquitos that carried malaria, which killed up to 3 million people a year worldwide. It was also used to stop other insect-borne diseases such as yellow fever, river blindness, elephantiasis, epidemic and

experience a "green revolution." Never before had so few farmers grown so much food for so many people. But as pesticide and herbicide use increased, insects and weeds developed resistance to the poisons. Beneficial animals, as well as rivers, lakes, and streams, were harmed by pesticides.

The chemical that had started it

A small plane sprays crops with insecticides. One of the most effective of the new insecticides was DDT; the product was used both on crops and in the home. Only after studies were conducted on DDT did people realize it was a harmful poison.

murine typhus, and bubonic plague. DDT was hailed as a great boon to mankind. It was "the atomic bomb of insecticides," and the "killer of killers." [70] Paul Müller won the Nobel Prize in physiology and medicine in 1948 for his rediscovery of DDT.

The chemical was cheap and easy to use. After the war, housewives were advised to spray their kitchens, bathrooms, mattresses, and even family pets to get rid of bedbugs, lice, ticks, and cockroaches. During the 1950s, DDT was one of the world's most widely used chemicals.

Scientists began to notice, however, that wherever DDT was used, it caused unexpected results. Entire ecosystems were disrupted. In Southeast Asia, mosquitos were replaced by a plague of caterpillars. The DDT had killed the wasps that ate the caterpillars, which kept their numbers down. It also weakened the eggshells of many kinds of birds that ate DDT-tainted insects and reptiles, preventing reproduction. In North America birds of prey such as peregrine falcons and ospreys disappeared. The skies were also empty of shorebirds whose diets depended on small creatures raised in chemical-fouled waters. And DDT killed off robins, chickadees, cardinals, and other familiar nesting birds.

There were no guidelines on how to use the chemical. Farmers sprayed massive amounts on their fields. Residue washed into rivers, lakes, and streams. The compound was left lying around in open sacks in barnyards and garages, where it was sometimes dumped in animal feed or water supplies. DDT breaks down very slowly, and scientists began to notice DDT accumulations in the fatty tissues of some farm animals. Cows that ate grass sprayed with DDT passed the chemical along to humans, especially women. Nursing mothers passed it to their infants.

DDT use went on unabated until 1962, when Rachel Carson's influential criticism, *Silent Spring*, was published. The book—researched in the fifties—warned the public about a future where no eagles soared in the sky. DDT was finally banned in the United States and Europe in 1972. It is still in use in developing countries.

The Technology Paradox

In the fifties, as in other times, technology proved to be a paradox. Chemical pesticides and fertilizers reduced hunger and killed insects that had plagued mankind since the dawn of time. On the other hand, increased chemical use fouled the air and water, killed beneficial animals, and was linked to increased cancer rates in humans.

The miracles in modern medicines were profound. But the popularity of cigarettes and alcohol, the deadliness of fifties automobiles, and nuclear fallout all boosted the death rate.

Using the destructive power of the atomic bomb to generate electricity was the work of twentieth-century nuclear magicians. But the radioactive waste and risk of nuclear accidents frightened people.

People in the fifties were just finding out that nothing from nature comes for free. Most people, however, went about their every day lives, cheered by the good things, and ignoring the downside as best they could. It would take the environmental movement of the early seventies to persuade Americans that balance was a fundamental aspect of nature.

Dwight D. Eisenhower welcomes successor John F. Kennedy to the White House in 1960. The election of the young, intelligent, and charismatic Kennedy revitalized the presidency.

Swinging into the Sixties

As the fifties drew to a close, the aging, frail Republican Dwight D. Eisenhower prepared to leave the presidency to Democrat John F. Kennedy. At forty-four, Kennedy was the youngest man yet elected to the office, and the image of the old World War II general passing the torch to a vibrant young man at the dawn of the sixties was a potent symbol.

America had been born of a dream of equality, liberty, and the pursuit of happiness. One hundred and seventy years later Americans still paid homage to those ideals. In retrospect the dream was not betrayed in the fifties, but it seemed trivialized. Possessions seemed more important than achievements. Order and conformity seemed more important than

A race rally conducted at Columbia University in 1968. The civil rights movement gained prominence in the 1960s.

Today, the fifties are painted in soft pastel images of safe neighborhoods and tailfinned cars, the sixties as a kind of abrupt aboutface, when revolution and rebellion transformed the "apathetic fifties" into the "swinging sixties." But the problems that existed in the sixties existed in the fifties. And the fact that they had been long ignored perhaps caused people to react more violently when they finally did react.

The fifties were predictable; few in that era foresaw the crisis and excitement that lay ahead in the sixties. But events in Little Rock, along with Beat poets and rock music, were portents of change.

Who could have foreseen that in the sixties:

the tiny civil rights and peace movements would grow so massively, that women would picket Miss America, that our creation of a puppet regime in South Vietnam would spark more than a decade of brutal Asian war, that college students and African Americans would riot, that DDT and other pesticides

freedom. The America of George Washington and Thomas Jefferson had become the America of McCarthy, Elvis, and Lucy.

would be found dangerous, that Presidents would be unmasked as crooks, that energy would be found to have its limits, that a few disaffected Beats would give rise to hippies, yippies, freaks, and flower children, and that rock and roll was here to stay? [71]

In 1959, according to Miller and Nowak, one establishment figure evaluating the youth of the fifties wrote about University of California students:

Employers are going to love this generation. They are going to be easy to handle. There aren't going to be any riots." Even as he spoke, his predictions were proving false. The times were (as Bob Dylan would soon tell us) a changin'. As early as 1958, 10,000 black and white students had come to Washington to participate in a "Youth March for Integrated Schools."[72] A year later, it was twenty thousand students.

Fifties practices such as nuclear testing, militarism, and compulsory military service would stir students to active protest. Groups like the Students for a Democratic Society (SDS) were formed in 1960, indicating a growing moral outrage in the young. This gave rise to the massive sit-in movement that was to follow.

It all began on February 1, 1960, when four black students sat down at a whites-only Woolworth lunch counter in Greensboro, North Carolina. They refused to move until they were served. This movement spread across the South until segregation was ended. (Dissatisfaction was not, however; one student said, "I sat-in at a restaurant for six months, and when they finally agreed to serve me, they didn't have what I wanted.") [73]

During this time, unknown to most Americans, consumer activist Ralph Nader was investigating auto safety and biologist Rachel Carson was amassing evidence against DDT. But the biggest change of the early sixties came on May 9, 1960, when the Food and Drug Administration quietly approved the first oral contaceptive for women—the birth control pill. The Pill quickly revolutionized relations between the sexes, freeing many women from the age-old fear of pregnancy. It set in motion a sexual revolution whose effects are still felt today.

The end of the decade was the beginning of a long youth rebellion. Writer H. Stuart Bell wrote approvingly, "For the more imaginative and sensitive men and women under thirty, ideology and utopia are far from dead.

During the 1963 March on Washington, thousands of citizens of all races joined together to protest the racist conditions under which blacks suffered.

They have suddenly and rather suprisingly come to life after ten blank years of slumber."[74]

From today's perspective we can see that it was the baby boomers—raised in the fifties—who initiated the modern movements for environmental, women's, and civil rights. Mistakes were made along the way. But there's no denying that the world as we see it today can be traced back, on a rather crooked line, to the decade of the 1950s.

Notes

Chapter One:
Superpowers and the Cold War

1. Quoted in David Halberstam, *The Fifties*. New York: Villard Books, 1993, p. 21.
2. Quoted in Halberstam, *The Fifties*, p. 22.
3. Quoted in Halberstam, *The Fifties*, p. 26.
4. Quoted in Halberstam, *The Fifties*, p. 29.
5. Quoted in Halberstam, *The Fifties*, p. 29.
6. Quoted in Halberstam, *The Fifties*, p. 48.
7. Quoted in David Wright and Elly Petra Press, *America in the 20th Century, 1950–1959*. New York: Marshall Cavendish, 1995, p. 800.
8. Quoted in Wright and Press, *America in the 20th Century*, p. 808.
9. Quoted in Halberstam, *The Fifties*, p. 62.
10. I. F. Stone, *The Haunted Fifties*. New York: Vintage Books, 1969, pp. 49–50.

Chapter Two:
The Cold War at Home

11. Quoted in Wright and Press, *America in the 20th Century*, p. 783.
12. Quoted in Wright and Press, *America in the 20th Century*, p. 783.
13. Halberstam, *The Fifties*, p. 336.
14. Quoted in Halberstam, *The Fifties*, p. 50.
15. Quoted in Halberstam, *The Fifties*, p. 49.
16. Quoted in Associated Press, *Twentieth Century America*, vol. 4, *The Cold War at Home and Abroad: 1945–1953*. New York: Grolier, 1995, p. 157.
17. Quoted in Halberstam, *The Fifties*, p. 55.
18. Quoted in Associated Press, *Twentieth Century America*, vol. 5, *The Eisenhower Years: 1952–1960*. New York: Grolier, 1995, p.53.
19. Quoted in Susan Jonas and Marilyn Nissenson, *Going, Going, Gone: Vanishing Americana*. San Francisco: Chronicle Books, 1994, p. 39.

20. Quoted in Jonas and Nissenson, *Going, Going, Gone*, p. 39.
21. Douglas T. Miller and Marion Nowak, *The Fifties: The Way We Really Were*. Garden City, NY: Doubleday, 1975, p. 35.
22. Quoted in Jim Hargrove, *Dwight D. Eisenhower*. Chicago: Childrens Press, 1987, p. 83.

Chapter Three:
The Struggle For Equality

23. Quoted in Miller and Nowak, *The Fifties*, p. 183
24. Quoted in Stuart A. Kallen, *The Civil Rights Movement*. Minneapolis, MN: Abdo & Daughters, 1990, p. 14.
25. Quoted in Stone, *The Haunted Fifties*, p. 61.
26. Quoted in Halberstam, *The Fifties*, p. 432.
27. Quoted in Halberstam, *The Fifties*, p. 433.
28. Quoted in Halberstam, *The Fifties*, p. 434.
29. Quoted in Halberstam, *The Fifties*, p. 435.
30. Quoted in Halberstam, *The Fifties*, p. 436.
31. Quoted in Halberstam, *The Fifties*, p. 441.
32. Quoted in Associated Press, *The Eisenhower Years*, p. 105.

Chapter Four:
Growing Up in the Fifties

33. Quoted in Miller and Nowak, *The Fifties*, p. 127.
34. Quoted in Miller and Nowak, *The Fifties*, p. 147.
35. Quoted in Miller and Nowak, *The Fifties*, p. 147.
36. Quoted in Miller and Nowak, *The Fifties*, p. 154.
37. *Grolier's Multimedia Encyclopedia*. Novato, CA: Mindscape, 1997.
38. Miller and Nowak, *The Fifties*, p. 271.
39. Quoted in Miller and Nowak, *The Fifties*, p. 269.
40. Quoted in Miller and Nowak, *The Fifties*, p. 273.
41. Quoted in Miller and Nowak, *The Fifties*, p. 274.

Chapter Five:
The Golden Age of Television

42. Quoted in Halberstam, *The Fifties*, p. 509.
43. Miller and Nowak, *The Fifties*, p. 348.
44. Quoted in J. Fred MacDonald, *One Nation Under Television*. New York: Pantheon, 1990, p. 82.
45. Quoted in MacDonald, *One Nation Under Television*, p. 83.
46. Quoted in MacDonald, *One Nation Under Television*, p. 86.

47. Quoted in MacDonald, *One Nation Under Television*, p. 86.
48. Quoted in Halberstam, *The Fifties*, p. 197.
49. Quoted in Halberstam, *The Fifties*, p. 198.
50. Quoted in Halberstam, *The Fifties*, p. 199.
51. Quoted in Halberstam, *The Fifties*, p. 200.
52. J. Fred MacDonald, *One Nation Under Television*, p. 107.

Chapter Six:
Rock, Writing, and Beatnik Rebellion

53. Quoted in Halberstam, *The Fifties*, p. 471.
54. Quoted in Associated Press, *The Eisenhower Years*, p. 172.
55. Quoted in Miller and Nowak, *The Fifties*, p. 307.
56. Quoted in Miller and Nowak, *The Fifties*, p. 308.
57. Quoted in Halberstam, *The Fifties*, p. 300.
58. Jack Kerouac, *The Lonesome Traveler*. New York: Grove Press, 1960, p. 105.
59. Kerouac, *The Lonesome Traveler*, unnumbered preface.
60. Halberstam, *The Fifties*, pp. 305-306.
61. Quoted in Halberstam, *The Fifties*, p. 306.

62. Quoted in Miller and Nowak, *The Fifties*, p. 385.
63. Quoted in Miller and Nowak, *The Fifties*, p. 387.
64. Miller and Nowak, *The Fifties*, p. 387.
65. Quoted in Halberstam, *The Fifties*, p. 307.

Chapter Seven:
Technology and Science

66. Quoted in Miller and Nowak, *The Fifties*, p. 48.
67. Quoted in Miller and Nowak, *The Fifties*, p. 49.
68. Quoted in William L. O'Neill, *American High: The Years of Confidence, 1945-1960*. New York: Free Press, 1986, p. 138.
69. Quoted in Miller and Nowak, *The Fifties*, pp. 131-132.
70. Quoted in Jonas and Nissenson, *Going, Going, Gone*, p. 42.

Epilogue:
Swinging Into the Sixties

71. Miller and Nowak, *The Fifties*, p. 395.
72. Miller and Nowak, *The Fifties*, p. 395.
73. Quoted in Kallen, *The Civil Rights Movement*, p. 44.
74. Quoted in Miller and Nowak, *The Fifties*, p. 398.

Chronology

1950

Census figures indicate U.S. population of 150,697,361.

January 31: President Harry Truman approves production of the hydrogen bomb.

February 9: Sen. Joseph McCarthy claims many in federal government are communists; his speech ushers in four years of red-baiting later known as the McCarthy era.

June 27: Truman sends air force and navy personnel to Korea after North Korea invades the south; ground forces are deployed three days later.

November 26: Chinese troops attack UN forces in Korea.

1951

Employment of women outside the home reaches peak of 19.3 million.

Supreme Court bars "subversives" from teaching in public schools.

March 29: Julius and Ethel Rosenberg found guilty of selling U.S. atomic secrets to the Soviet Union and are sentenced to death.

July: Korean cease-fire talks begin and last two years.

September 4: Transcontinental television begins with a speech by President Truman.

Fall: J. D. Salinger' *Catcher in the Rye* is published.

1952

TV Guide magazine is founded.

November 1: The first hydrogen bomb is exploded by the United States.

November 4: Dwight D. Eisenhower is elected president.

1953

First hydrogen bomb is exploded by the Soviet Union.

Earl Warren appointed chief justice of the Supreme Court, ushering in an era of court-ordered civil rights victories for African Americans.

March 5: Soviet dictator Joseph Stalin dies.

June 19: Ethel and Julius Rosenberg die in the electric chair.

July 27: Fighting ends in Korea.

1954

Nuclear fallout problem widely debated.

Construction of the St. Lawrence Seaway begins.

Salk polio vaccine is developed.

January 21: The first atomic-powered submarine, *Nautilus,* is launched in Groton, Connecticut.

May 17: Supreme Court orders school desegregation and declares "separate but equal" schools unconstitutional in landmark case, *Brown v. Board of Education.*

April 22: McCarthy begins nationally televised hearings on U.S. Army, which initiate McCarthy's downfall.

December 22: Senate votes 67-22 to censure McCarthy for his behavior during the Army-McCarthy hearings.

1955

United States formally ends World War II–era occupation of Germany.

First presidential press conference filmed for TV.

Bill Haley and the Comets have number-one hit, "Rock Around the Clock."

Tranquilizers come into widespread use.

March 31: Supreme Court orders public schools integrated with "all deliberate speed."

September 30: Actor James Dean is killed in a car accident.

December 1: Rosa Parks refuses to give up her seat on a Montgomery, Alabama bus; her arrest prompts a boycott that overturns segregation and Jim Crow laws.

1956

January 30: Rev. Martin Luther King Jr. urges nonviolence after his house is firebombed during the Montgomery bus boycott.

March 12: More than one hundred U.S. congressmen call for resistance to Supreme Court–ordered desegregation.

April 21: Elvis Presley has first number one-hit, "Heartbreak Hotel."

June 29: Federal Interstate Highway Act is signed, marking the beginning of a extensive interstate highway building program.

October 23: Hungarians begin massive protests in the streets of Budapest against Soviet occupation.

1957

April 29: Voting rights are confirmed for African Americans when Congress passes a civil rights bill.

September 4: Arkansas National Guardsmen prevent nine black children from entering Little Rock's Central High.

September 24: Eisenhower sends federal troops to Arkansas to provide safe passage into Central High for the Little Rock Nine.

Fall: Jack Kerouac's *On the Road* is published.

October 5: Soviet Union launches *Sputnik*, the first satellite in space.

1958

Nikita Khrushchev becomes premier of Soviet Union.

January 31: First U.S. satellite, *Explorer*, successfully orbits the earth.

March 24: Elvis Presley enters the U.S. Army.

December 10: The first domestic jet airline passenger service begins between New York City and Miami.

1959

January 1: Fidel Castro becomes dictator of Cuba.

January 3: Alaska becomes the forty-ninth state.

August 21: Hawaii becomes the fiftieth state.

September 15–27: Nikita Khrushchev visits the United States, but is barred from going to Disneyland for security reasons.

For Further Reading

Tom Bower, *The Paperclip Conspiracy: The Hunt for Nazi Scientists*. Boston: Little, Brown, 1987. A well-researched book that reveals the high crimes of many Nazi German scientists who were brought to America in the 1950s. Gives detailed information on the white-wash of the backgrounds of people like Wernher von Braun.

Paul Boyer, *By the Bomb's Early Light: American Thought and Culture at the Dawn of the Atomic Age*. New York: Pantheon, 1985. A highly original work of cultural history that explores the cultural fallout of the atom bomb. Boyer uses a wealth of cartoons, opinion polls, radio shows, movies, slang, song lyrics, and other evidence to show how the bomb penetrated the fabric of American life.

Warren French, *San Francisco Poetry Renaissance: 1955–1960*. Boston: Twayne, 1991. An overview of the Beat poetry renaissance starting with Ginsberg's reading of *Howl* in 1956. Covers famous and not-so-famous Beat poets of the fifties.

Allen Ginsberg, *Collected Poems 1947–1980*. New York: Perennial Library, 1988. The great poems of Beat poet Allen Ginsberg.

David Halberstam, *The Fifties*. New York: Villard Books, 1993. The definitive, eight-hundred-page history of the fifties by renowned journalist David Halberstam. Details the personalities and backgrounds of prominent men and women who shaped fifties history.

Brett Harvey, ed., *The Fifties: A Woman's Oral History*. New York: HarperCollins, 1993. Details the hopes, thoughts, and fears of women who lived through the fifties. Filled with moving and revealing stories of many women speaking in their own words, this book offers deep insight into the way things really were in the fifties.

Walter L. Hixton, *Parting the Curtain: Propaganda, Culture, and the Cold War*. New York: St. Martin's Press, 1997. An account of the propaganda war waged by the U.S. government in which the weapons were Coke, Cadillacs, and fashion models. A beautifully researched book on how these images were broadcast into the Soviet Union to foment revolution by showing communists the American way.

Susan Jonas and Marilyn Nissenson, *Going, Going, Gone: Vanishing Americana.* San Francisco: Chronicle Books, 1994. A large collection of pictures and essays that speak about the rise and fall of many fifties fads and institutions. These funny and not-so-funny pages include the rise and fall of polio scares, balsa-wood model airplanes, rotary phones, automats, black-and-white movies, and more.

Stuart A. Kallen, *The Civil Rights Movement.* Minneapolis, MN: Abdo & Daughters, 1990. A history of the African American struggle for equality from 1946 to 1970.

Stuart A. Kallen, *Roots of Rock.* Vol. 2. Minneapolis, MN: Abdo & Daughters, 1989. Delves into the rise of rock music in the late fifties.

Jack Kerouac, *On the Road.* New York: Viking, 1957. The story of a generation of young men roaming America after World War II in a wild, desperate search for identity and purpose. An essential book for anyone inter-ested in the Beat generation.

J. Fred MacDonald, *One Nation Under Television.* New York: Pantheon, 1990. An excellent history of fifty years of American television written by a professor at Northwestern and the curator of the Chicago Museum of Broadcast Communications. Full of primary source quotations and fascinating statistics. Recommended for anyone interested in television.

Douglas T. Miller and Marion Nowak, *The Fifties: The Way We Really Were.* Garden City, NY: Doubleday, 1975. An in-depth social and cultural history of the fifties from a slightly cynical point of view.

Kevin Rafferty, producer, *The Atomic Café.* New York: New Yorker Films, 1982. A wonderful—if chilling—film comprised of army propaganda films, newsreels, commercials, and other footage. Backed by funny fifties songs such as "Fighting the Cold War with You" and "When Atom Bombs Fall," the film suggests the stark reality of life under the nuclear shadow.

Works Consulted

Associated Press, *Twentieth Century America*. Vol. 4, *The Cold War at Home and Abroad: 1945–1953*. New York: Grolier, 1995. A detailed account of late forties and early fifties history taken directly from Associated Press newspaper stories written as the news was unfolding.

Associated Press, *Twentieth Century America*. Vol. 5, *The Eisenhower Years: 1952–1960*. New York: Grolier, 1995. Another book of fifties history torn from the pages of Associated Press notebooks, this one covering the Eisenhower years.

William Boddy, *Fifties Television*. Chicago: University of Illinois Press, 1990. Assesses the golden age of television and gives fresh insight into the power of this invention.

Reuven Frank, *Out of Thin Air*. New York: Simon & Schuster, 1991. A history of television network news.

Jim Hargrove, *Harry S. Truman* and *Dwight D. Eisenhower*. Chicago: Childrens Press, 1987. Two books written for junior high school readers that detail the lives of the two fifties presidents.

Arleen Keylin, ed., *The Fabulous Fifties*. New York: Arno Press, 1978. A book of photos and reprints of the front page of the *New York Times* in a year-by-year breakdown of the fifties.

William E. Leuchtenburg and the Editors of *Life*, *The Great Age of Change*. New York: Time, 1964. A detailed account of the politics and history of the fifties.

Peter Lewis, *The Fifties*. New York: J. B. Lippincott, 1978. Written by a well-known British journalist, this book gives a view of fifties America from an English perspective.

William L. O'Neill, *American High: The Years of Confidence, 1945–1960*. New York: Free Press, 1986. Written from the perspective that the fifties was a time of confidence and good feeling, this work analyzes the reasons for that "American high."

I. F. Stone, *The Haunted Fifties*. New York: Vintage, 1969. Collected columns by visionary fifties writer I. F. Stone, who paints a critical picture of fifties cold war mentality.

David Wright and Elly Petra Press, *America in the 20th Century, 1950–1959*. New York: Marshall Cavendish, 1995. A book for young adults that discusses life in the fifties; abundant photographs.

Index

Picture Credits

Cover photos: (From left to right) APA/Archive Photos, UPI/Corbis-Bettmann, Archive Photos

American Stock/Archive Photos, 33
AP/Wide World Photos, 25, 42, 79
AP Photo/Gene Herrick, 48
AP Photo/Files, 51
Archive Photos, 8, 18, 23, 60, 80, 89, 96, 102, 109
Archive Photos/American Stock, 59
Archive Photos/Michael Barson, 21
Neal Boenzi/New York Times Co./Archive Photos, 110
Camerique/Archive Photos, 55
H. S. Capman/Corbis-Bettmann, 87
Corbis, 57
Corbis-Bettmann, 73
Daily Mirror/Corbis, 91

© Digital Stock, 52, 53, 94
Express Newspapers/Archive Photos, 37
Lambert/Archive Photos, 4
Library of Congress, 47, 50, 65, 99, 103, 104, 112
National Archives, 5, 16, 17, 26, 34, 100
Pach/Corbis-Bettmann, 9
Official U.S. Navy Photograph, 6
Photofest, 68, 70, 71, 75, 76, 78, 81, 82, 83
Schomburg Center for Research in Black Culture, 36, 39
© Smithsonian Institution, 14
UPI/Corbis-Bettmann, 7, 12, 20, 28, 29, 41, 44, 63, 67, 85, 92, 95, 106
USDA/APHIS, 107

About the Author

Stuart A. Kallen was born in 1955, the day Chuck Berry's "Maybellene" was number one. He is the author of more than 125 nonfiction books for children and young adults. He has written on fifties topics ranging from Soviet history to rock 'n' roll to the civil rights movement. Mr. Kallen lives in San Diego, California, where the fifties are long gone.